Wiring and Lighting

CHRIS KITCHER

THE CROWOOD PRESS

First published in 2012 by
The Crowood Press Ltd
Ramsbury, Marlborough
Wiltshire SN8 2HR

enquiries@crowood.com

www.crowood.com

New edition 2020

This impression 2022

British Library Cataloguing-in-Publication Data
A catalogue record for this book is available from the
British Library.

ISBN 978 1 78500 743 9

Disclaimer
The author and the publisher do not accept any
responsibility in any manner whatsoever for any
error or omission, or any loss, damage, injury, adverse
outcome, or liability of any kind incurred as a result of
the use of any of the information contained in this book,
or reliance upon it.

Unless otherwise stated, all photographs and drawings
are by the author.

Typeset and designed by D & N Publishing
Baydon, Wiltshire

Printed and bound in India by Replika Press Pvt Ltd

ABBREVIATIONS

CPC	Circuit Protective Conductor
CSA	Cross Sectional Area
DNO	District Network Operator
FELV	Functional Extra-Low Voltage
Isc	Short Circuit Current
LSF	Low Smoke Thermoplastic
MICC	Mineral Insulated Metal Clad Cable
PEFC	Prospective Earth Fault Current Test
PELV	Protected Extra-Low Voltage
PIR	Passive Infra-red Detector
PME	Protective Multiple Earthing
PSCC	Prospective Short Circuit Current Test
PV	Photovoltaic System
RCBO	Residual Current Device with Overload Protection
RCD	Residual Current Device
SELV	Separated Extra-Low Voltage
SWA	Steel Wired Armoured
Voc	Open Circuit Voltage

Contents

1	Important Information	4
2	Working Safely	19
3	Tools and Equipment	24
4	Voltage Bands	27
5	Dealing with Cables	30
6	Installation Methods	45
7	Planning an Electrical Job	66
8	Protective Earthing and Bonding, and Supply Systems	75
9	Wiring of Lighting Circuits	91
10	Power Circuits	113
11	Cable Selection	129
12	Photovoltaic Microgeneration Systems	134
13	Inspection, Testing and Certification	142
Index		159

CHAPTER I

Important Information

INTRODUCTION

Before commencing any type of work on or around an electrical installation, it is very important to know and understand the legal requirements to which all of us must comply. These requirements apply to all who are involved in electrical work, whether it is a very large electrical contracting company working on commercial or industrial installations, or a DIY enthusiast carrying out very small electrical jobs at home.

Electricity can be very dangerous if it is not dealt with in the correct manner and this is why we have rules and regulations, which we must be aware of before picking up our tools to start work.

LEGAL REQUIREMENTS

The Health and Safety at Work Act 1979 (HASAWA) is a statutory document to which we must all comply; failure to comply with a statutory document is a criminal offence. HASAWA can be considered to be the umbrella, under which all of the other documents sit. The Electricity at Work Regulations 1989 (EAWR) is in place to provide the requirements for the safety of electrical installations and is also a statutory document.

This book is intended to provide information to anyone who is carrying out work on a domestic installation. Since 2005, electrical work carried out in domestic dwellings has been included in the building regulations and is known as building regulation part P. It is a legal requirement to comply with building regulations and failure to do so may result in a fine or even imprisonment.

Clearly, anyone who simply wants to carry out a small electrical job on their own property does not want to get wrapped up in too many rules and regulations, but it would be silly for us to ignore them. Imagine what the implications would be if we were to carry out electrical work that did not comply with the requirements and somebody got electrocuted or a building was damaged, possibly due to fire caused by a poor electrical installation. I am sure that house insurers would not be keen on paying out to repair any damage that was caused by poor workmanship; they would also not pay out for any damage caused by work that was carried out illegally. To ensure that this does not happen we must have a basic understanding of the rules to which we must work.

It is not a requirement to be qualified to carry out electrical work but we must be competent. The definition of a competent person is:

> A person who possesses sufficient technical knowledge, relevant practical skills and experience for the nature of the electrical work undertaken and is able at all times to prevent danger and, where appropriate, injury to him/herself and others.

You will be the best person to decide if you fit that definition or not!

The important things to be aware of are:

- All electrical work carried out must be in

compliance with the current British Standard, which is BS 7671 Requirements for Electrical Installation. At the time of writing this book, the current standard is the 18th edition 2019.

- Compliance with this requires that all installed equipment and materials used are also to a British or suitable European standard. Of course there will be occasions where we need to install a piece of equipment that does not have a BS standard. An example of this could be if you have had a lamp made by a local blacksmith that you want to install as an outside light – the lamp will not have a British standard. In these situations you will need to make a judgement as to whether the lamp would be likely to meet the requirements of the British standard; in other words, will it be safe? As long as you are satisfied that it is safe and suitable for the use to which it is being put, it can be fitted; the only requirement is that the item is recorded as not being to a British standard on whatever certificate you need to complete for the particular job. The use of certificates will be covered in detail later in this book.

BUILDING REGULATIONS

Electrical installations must also comply with all of the relevant building regulations; this is a legal requirement. Building regulations are identified by the use of letters and they run from parts A through to P (though there is no part O). Of course, none of these building regulations are more important than any other; however, part P will have to be complied with along with all other requirements when considering carrying out electrical work in dwellings.

BUILDING REGULATION PART P

Because electrical installations in domestic dwellings are covered by building regulation part P, we have to be aware of what the requirements are.

First, regardless of what we are permitted to do, all parts of any electrical work that we carry out have to be in compliance with the latest edition of BS 7671 Electrical Wiring Regulations.

In most cases, part P requires us to notify building control of any electrical work that is being carried out. However, we are permitted, without notifying our local building control department, to add to an existing circuit; for example, this could be an additional lighting point or an additional socket outlet. We are also allowed to replace a damaged circuit, providing that the cable that we use is the same size and follows the same route as the original circuit. We would not, however, be permitted to change the rating or the type of protective device for any circuit. All work that is carried out must be inspected and tested correctly and the appropriate certification provided. The use and completion of different types of certification will be explained in detail late in this book.

NEW CIRCUITS

All new circuits, other than a single replacement, will be need to be notified to the local building control department, which will require the completion of a building notice and the payment of a fee. The building control officer will usually want to come out and inspect the work at each stage. Certainly he will want to inspect any parts of the installation that will not be visible to him once the work has been completed. Although the building inspector will inspect the various stages of the installation, it is the responsibility of the person carrying out the installation to provide the correct certification on completion of the work. As previously stated, it is not a requirement to be qualified to carry out any type of electrical work; however, it may be that the building control officer will need to be satisfied that you are competent enough to carry out and certificate on completion the work that you intend to carry out.

All work carried out in a bathroom or a kitchen must be notified to building control; this is regardless of whether it is an addition or alteration to an existing circuit or whether it is a new circuit. Circuits installed to provide electricity to sheds and remote buildings are also notifiable.

Most electricians who are involved in domestic electrical installations will join a self-certification scheme and become a part P registered domestic

Certification of Electrical Work

It is a requirement of part P that all work carried out in a domestic dwelling is certificated, and, of course, it is very important that the correct type of certification is completed.

For alterations to an existing circuit, where the protective device remains unchanged, the correct certificate to be used is a Minor Electrical Installation Works Certificate. commonly known as a Minor Works Certificate.

Megger.

Certificate No:	0

MINOR ELECTRICAL INSTALLATION WORKS CERTIFICATE
(REQUIREMENTS FOR ELECTRICAL INSTALLATIONS - BS7671 [IET WIRING REGULATIONS])
To be used only for minor electrical work which does not include the provision of a new circuit.

PART 1: Description of the minor works

1. Details of the Client   Date minor works completed

2. Location/Address

3. Description of the minor works

4. Details of departures, if any, from BS7671:2018 for the circuit altered or extended (Regulation 120.3, 133.1.3 and 133.5)
Where applicable, a suitable risk assessment(s) must be attached to this Certificate.

Risk assessment attached ☐

5. Comments on (including any defects observed in) the existing installation (Regulation 644.1.2):

PART 2: Presence and adequacy of installation earthing and bonding arrangements (Regulation 132.16)

1. System earthing arrangement   TN-S ☐   TN-C-S ☐   TT ☐

2. Earth fault loop impedance at distribution board (Z_{db}) supplying the final circuit Ω

3. Presence of adequate main protective conductors:

     Earthing conductor ☐

     Main protective bonding conductor(s) to: Water ☐   Gas ☐   Oil ☐   Structured steel ☐   Other   ☐

PART 3: Circuit details

DB Reference No: DB Location and type:
Circuit No: Circuit Description:
Circuit overcurrent protective device: BS(EN)   Type   Rating   A
Conductor sizes: Live   mm^2 cpc   mm^2

PART 4: Test results for the circuit altered or extended (where relevent and practicable)

Protective conductor continuity: R1 + R2 Ω or   R2 Ω
Continuity of ring final circuit conductors: L/L Ω N/N Ω cpc/cpc Ω
Insulation resistance: Live-Live   MΩ Live-Earth   MΩ
Polarity satisfactory ☐   Maximum measured earth fault loop impedance: Z_s Ω
RCD operation: Rated residual operating current ($I_{\Delta n}$)   mA
Disconnection time   ms
Satisfactory test button operation ☐

PART 5: Declaration

I certify that the work covered by this certificate does not impair the safety of the existing installation and the work have been designed, constructed, inspected and tested in accordance with BS7671:2018 (IET Wiring Regulations) amended to and that to the best of my knowledge and belief, at the time of my inspection, complied with BS7671 except as detailed in Part 1 above.

Name: Signature:
For and on behalf of:
Address:
     Position:
     Date:

This form was developed by Megger Limited and is based on the model shown in Appendix 6 of BS 7671 : 2018. © Megger Limited 2018

Page 1 of 2

Certification of Electrical Work *continued*

Megger.

MINOR ELECTRICAL INSTALLATION WORKS CERTIFICATE
GUIDANCE FOR RECIPIENTS (to be appended to the certificate)

This Certificate has been issued to confirm that the electrical installation work to which it relates has been designed, constructed, inspected and tested in accordance with British Standard 7671 (the IET Wiring Regulations).

You should have received an "original" Certificate and the contractor should have retained a duplicate. If you were the person ordering the work, but not the owner of the installation, you should pass this Certificate, or a copy of it, to the owner. A separate Certificate should have been received for each existing circuit on which minor works have been carried out. This Certificate is not appropriate if you requested the contractor to undertake more extensive installation work, for which you should have received an Electrical Installation Certificate.

The Certificate should be retained in a safe place and be shown to any person inspecting or undertaking further work on the electrical installation in the future. If you later vacate the property, this Certificate will demonstrate to the new owner that the minor electrical installation work carried out complied with the requirements of British Standard 7671 at the time the Certificate was issued.

installer, this would allow them to carry out work and certify it without completing a building notice for each job carried out. To become a registered installer you would need to contact your chosen scheme provider, who will send you details of their registration requirements. All registration bodies will require a fee. Once it is paid they will arrange to visit you, inspect your quality-management system and also look at some of your work.

ELECTRICAL INSTALLATION CERTIFICATE

An electrical installation certificate needs to be completed for all new installations, additions to existing installations and alterations to an existing installation. This certificate should not be issued unless the installation meets all of the requirements of BS7671.

A new installation would be a new electrical system installed into a new building or it could be a rewire of an existing installation. An addition of a new installation would be when a new circuit has been installed to an existing installation; this would also require the completion of an electrical installation certificate for the work carried out. A single installation that has been added to over a period of time, may have several electrical installation certificates. It is not permissible to add details to an existing certificate.

Alterations would be where, perhaps, the consumer's unit has been changed along with the type of protective devices, or where circuit breakers have been replaced with RCBOs. In these instances, the electrical installation certificate is used to describe these alterations, and to indicate that the altered areas of the electrical system are compliant with the latest edition of the wiring regulations BS7671.

Wherever an electrical installation certificate is used, it must be accompanied by a schedule of test results and a schedule of inspections. Again these documents must give information on the work that has just been carried out, not information on existing circuits. This, of course, will in some cases result in some installations having several of these documents, which have been provided over a period of time.

Before undertaking any work on an existing installation, it must first be ascertained that the installation is safe to add to. In some instances this will require the completion of an electrical installation condition report.

Megger.

ELECTRICAL INSTALLATION CERTIFICATE

(REQUIREMENTS FOR ELECTRICAL INSTALLATIONS BS7671 [IET WIRING REGULATIONS])

DETAILS OF THE CLIENT
Client:
Address:

INSTALLATION ADDRESS
Occupier:
Address:

DESCRIPTION AND EXTENT OF THE INSTALLATION

Description of Installation

New installation	☐
Addition to an existing installation	☐
Alteration to an existing installation	☐

Extent of installation covered by this Certificate:

(use continuation sheet if necessary)   see continuation sheet No:

FOR DESIGN, CONSTRUCTION, INSPECTION AND TESTING

I being the person responsible for the Design, Construction, Inspection & Testing of the electrical installation (as indicated by my signature below), particulars of which are described above, having exercised reasonable skill and care when carrying out that Design, Construction, Inspection & Testing, hereby CERTIFY that the design work for which I have been responsible is to the best of my knowledge and belief in accordance with BS7671: 2018 amended to   except for any departures, if any, detailed as follows.
Details of departures from BS7671 (Regulations 120.3 and 133.5):

Details of permitted exceptions (Regulation 411.3.3). Where applicable, a suitable risk assessment(s) must be attached to this certificate.

Risk assessment attached ☐

The extent of liability of the signatory is limited to the work described above as the subject of this Certificate.
Name (IN BLOCK LETTERS)   Date:
    Company: Chris Kitcher
    Address: 14 Ockenden Way
                               Signature:

                              Tel No:
            Hassocks

NEXT INSPECTION
I the designer, recommend that this installation is further inspected and tested after an interval of not more than

Page 1 of 6

This form was developed by Megger Limited and is based on the model shown
in Appendix 6 of BS7671 : 2018   © Megger Limited 2018

Electrical installation certificate.

SUPPLY CHARACTERISTICS AND EARTHING ARRANGEMENTS

Earthing arrangements

TN-C ☐
TN-S ☐
TN-C-S ☐
TT ☐
IT ☐

Other source of supply (as detailed on attached schedule)

Number and Type of Live Conductors

AC ☐   DC ☐
1-Phase,2-Wire ☐   2-wire ☐
2-Phase,3-Wire ☐   3-wire ☐
3-Phase,3-Wire ☐   Other ☐
3-Phase,4-Wire ☐

Confirmation of supply polarity ☐

Nature of Supply Parameters

Nominal voltage, U/U_0 [(1)] _____ V

Nominal frequency, f (1) _____ Hz

Prospective fault current, I_{pf} [(2)] _____ kA

External loop impedance, Z_e [(2)] _____ Ω

(Note: (1) by enquiry, (2) by enquiry or by measurement)

Supply Protective Device Characteristics

BS (EN)

Type

Rated Current _____ A

PARTICULARS OF INSTALLATION REFERRED TO IN THE CERTIFICATE

Means of Earthing

Distributor's Facility ☐

Installation Earth Electrode ☐

Maximum Demand

Maximum demand (load)

Details of installation Earth Electrode: *(where applicable)*

Type: *(e.g. rod(s), tape etc)*   Location: Electrode resistance to earth:
_____ Ω

Main Protective Conductors

Earthing Conductor	Material	csa _____ mm²	Connection / continuity verified ☐
Main protective bonding conductors (to extraneous-conductive-parts)	Material	csa _____ mm²	Connection / continuity verified ☐

To water installation pipes ☐	To gas installation pipes ☐	To oil installation pipes ☐	To structural steel ☐

To lightning protection ☐   To other ☐   Specify

Main Switch / Switch-Fuse / Circuit-Breaker / RCD

Location:
BS, Type:
No of poles:

Current rating: _____ A
Fuse / device rating or setting: _____ A
Voltage rating: _____ V

If RCD main switch

Rated residual operating current $I_{\Delta n}$ _____ mA
Rated time delay _____ ms
Measured operating time _____ ms

COMMENTS ON EXISTING INSTALLATION   *(in the case of an alteration or additions see Regulation 644.1.2):*

SCHEDULES

The attached schedules are part of this document and this Certificate is valid only when they are attached to it.

_____ Schedules of Inspections and _____ Schedules of Test Results are attached.

(Enter quantities of schedules attached)

Certificate No: 2

SCHEDULE OF INSPECTIONS (for new installation work only) for DOMESTIC AND SIMILAR PREMISES WITH UP TO 100 A SUPPLY

NOTE 1: This form is suitable for many types of smaller installation not exclusively domestic.

All items inspected in order to confirm, as appropriate, compliance with the relevent clauses in BS7671. The list of items and associated examples where given are not exhaustive.

NOTE 2: Insert ✓ to indicate an inspection has been carried out and the result is satisfactory, or N/A to indicate that the inspection is not applicable to a particular item.

ITEM NO	DESCRIPTION	OUTCOME See Note 2
1.0	**EXTERNAL CONDITION OF INTAKE EQUIPMENT (VISUAL INSPECTION ONLY)**	
1.1	Service cable	
1.2	Service head	
1.3	Earthing arrangement	
1.4	Meter tails	
1.5	Metering equipment	
1.6	Isolator (where present)	
2.0	**PARALLEL OR SWITCHED ALTERNATIVE SOURCES OF SUPPLY**	
2.1	Adequate arrangements where a generating set operates as a switched alternative to the public supply (551.6)	
2.2	Adequate arrangements where a generating set operates in parallel with the public supply (551.7)	
3.0	**AUTOMATIC DISCONNECTION OF SUPPLY**	
3.1	**Presence and adequacy of earthing and protective bonding arrangements:**	
	• Distributor's earthing arrangement (542.1.2.1; 542.1.2.2)	
	• Installation earth electrode (where applicable) (542.1.2.3)	
	• Earthing conductor and connections, including accessibility (542.3; 543.3.2)	
	• Main protective bonding conductors and connections including accessibility (411.3.1.2; 543.3.2; 544.1)	
	• Provision of safety electrical earthing / bonding labels at all appropriate locations (514.13)	
	• RCD(s) provided for fault protection (411.4.204; 411.5.3)	
4.0	**BASIC PROTECTION**	
4.1	**Presence and adequacy of measures to provide basic protection (prevention of contact with live parts) within the installation:**	
	• Insulation of live parts e.g. conductors completely covered with durable insulating materials (416.1)	
	• Barriers or enclosures e.g. correct IP rating (416.2)	
5.0	**ADDITIONAL PROTECTION**	
5.1	**Presence and effectiveness of additional protection methods:**	
	• RCD(s) not exceeding 30 mA operating current (415.1; Part 7), see item 8.14 of this schedule	
	• Supplementary bonding (415.2; Part 7)	
6.0	**OTHER METHODS OF PROTECTION**	
6.1	**Presence and effectiveness of methods which give both basic and fault protection:**	
	• SELV systems, including the source and associated circuits (414)	
	• PELV systems, including the source and associated circuits (414)	
	• Double or reinforced insulation i.e. Class II or equivalent equipment and associated circuits (412)	
	• Electrical separation for one item of equipment e.g. shaver supply unit (413)	
7.0	**CONSUMER UNIT(S) / DISTRIBUTION BOARD(S):**	
7.1	Adequacy of access and working space for items of electrical equipment including switchgear (132.12)	
7.2	Components are suitable according to assembly manufacturer's instructions or literature (536.4.203)	
7.3	Presence of linked main switch(es) (462.1.201)	
7.4	Isolators, for every circuit or group of circuits and all items of equipment (462.2)	
7.5	Suitability of enclosure(s) for IP and fire ratings (416.2; 421.1.6; 421.1.201; 526.5)	
7.6	Protection against mechanical damage where cables enter equipment (522.8.1; 522.8.5; 522.8.11)	
7.7	Confirmation that ALL conductor connections are correctly located in terminals and are tight and secure (526.1)	

First page of the Schedule of Inspections; the full Schedule can be seen on pp.146–147.

Certificate No: 2

ITEM NO	DESCRIPTION	OUTCOME See Note 2
7.0	**CONSUMER UNIT(S) / DISTRIBUTION BOARD (S) continued**	
7.8	Avoidance of heating effects where cables enter ferromagnetic enclosures e.g. steel (521.5)	
7.9	Selection of correct type and ratings of circuit protective devices for overcurrent and fault protection (411.3.2; 411.4, 411.5, 411.6; 432, 433; 537.3.1.1)	
7.10	**Presence of appropriate circuit charts, warning and other notices:**	
	• Provision of circuit charts/schedules or equivalent forms of information (514.9)	
	• Warning notice of method of isolation where live parts not capable of being isolated by a single device (514.11)	
	• Periodic inspection and testing notice (514.12.1)	
	• RCD six-monthly test notice; where required (514.12.2)	
	• AFDD six-monthly test notice; where required	
	• Warning notice of non-standard (mixed) colours of conductors present (514.14)	
7.11	Presence of labels to indicate the purpose of switchgear and protective devices (514.1.1; 514.8)	
8.0	**CIRCUITS**	
8.1	Adequacy of conductors for current-carrying capacity with regard to type and nature of the installation (523)	
8.2	Cable installation methods suitable for the location(s) and external influences (522)	
8.3	Segregation/separation of Band I (ELV) and Band II (LV) circuits, and electrical and non-electrical services (528)	
8.4	Cables correctly erected and supported throughout including escape routes, with protection against abrasion (521, 522)	
8.5	Provision of fire barriers, sealing arrangements where necessary (527.2)	
8.6	Non-sheathed cables enclosed throughout in conduit, ducting or trunking (521.10.1; 526.8)	
8.7	Cables concealed under floors, above ceilings or in walls / partitions, adequately protected against damage (522.6.201; 522.6.202, 522.6.203, 522.6.204)	
8.8	Conductors correctly identified by colour, lettering or numbering (514)	
8.9	Presence, adequacy and correct termination of protective conductors (411.3.1.1; 543.1)	
8.10	Cables and conductors correctly connected, enclosed and with no undue mechanical strain (526)	
8.11	No basic insulation of a conductor visible outside enclosure (526.8)	
8.12	Single-pole devices for switching or protection in line conductors only (132.14.1; 530.3.3; 643.6)	
8.13	Accessories not damaged, securely fixed, correctly connected, suitable for external influences (134.1.1;512.2; Section 526)	
8.14	**Provision of additional protection by RCD not exceeding 30mA:**	
	• Socket-outlets rated at 32 A or less, unless exempt (411.3.3)	
	• Supplies for Mobile equipment with a current rating not exceeding 32 A for use outdoors (411.3.3)	
	• Cables concealed in walls at a depth of less than 50 mm (522.6.202; 522.6.203)	
	• Cables concealed in walls / partitions containing metal parts regardless of depth (522.6.202; 522.6.203)	
	• Final circuits supplying luminaires within domestic (household) premises (411.3.4)	
8.15	**Presence of appropriate devices for isolation and switching correctly located including:**	
	• Means of switching off for mechanical maintenance (Section 464; 537.3.2)	
	• Emergency switching (465.1; 537.3.3)	
	• Functional switching, for control of parts of the installation and current-using equipment (463.1; 537.3.1)	
	• Firefighter's switches (537.4)	
9.0	**CURRENT-USING EQUIPMENT (PERMANENTLY CONNECTED)**	
9.1	Equipment not damaged, securely fixed and suitable for external influences (134.1.1; 416.2; 512.2)	
9.2	Provision of overload and/or undervoltage protection e.g. for rotating machines, if required (Sections 445; 552)	
9.3	Installed to minimize the build-up of heat and restrict the spread of fire (421.1.4; 559.4.1)	
9.4	Adequacy of working space. Accessibility to equipment (132.12; 513.1)	
10.0	**LOCATION(S) CONTAINING A BATH OR SHOWER (SECTION 701)**	
10.1	30 mA RCD protection for all LV circuits, equipment suitable for the zones, supplementary bonding (where required) etc.	
11.0	**OTHER PART 7 SPECIAL INSTALLATIONS OR LOCATIONS**	
11.1	List all other special installations or locations present, if any. (Record separately the results of particular inspections applied)	

Inspected by:

Name (Capitals)   Signature   Date

GENERIC SCHEDULE OF TEST RESULTS

Certificate No: 1

DB reference no
Location
Zs at DB Ω
I_pf at DB (kA)
Correct supply polarity confirmed
Phase sequence confirmed (where appropriate)

Details of circuits and/or installed equipment vulnerable to damage when testing

Details of test instruments used (state serial and/or asset numbers)
Continuity
Insulation resistance
Earth fault loop impedance
RCD
Earth electrode resistance

Tested by:
Name (Capitals)
Signature
Date

Circuit Details													Test results												
	Circuit Description	Protective device						Conductor details			Ring final circuit continuity Ω			Continuity Ω (R1 + R2) or R2		Insulation Resistance			Polarity	Maximum measured Zs Ω	RCD		AFDD	Remarks (continue on a seperate sheet if necessary)
Circuit number		BS (EN)	type	rating (A)	breaking capacity (kA)	RCD I Δn (mA)	Maximum permitted Zs (Ω·)	Reference Method	Live (mm2)	cpc (mm2)	r1 (line)	rn (neutral)	r2 (cpc)	(R1 + R2)	R2	Test Voltage V	Live - Live	Live - Earth			Disconnection time (ms)	RCD test button operation	Manual AFDD test button operation	
1	2	3	4	5	6	7	8	9	10	11	12	13	14	15	16	17	18	19	20	21	22	23	24	25

* Where the maximum permitted earth fault loop impedance value stated in column 8 is taken from a source other than the tabulated values given in Chapter 41 of this Standard, state the source of the data in the appropriate cell for the circuit in the 'Remarks' column (column 25) of the schedule.

Schedule of test results.

ELECTRICAL INSTALLATION CONDITION REPORT

An electrical installation condition report is a document that is completed to provide information on the condition of an electrical installation.

All domestic installations should be subjected to a condition report at intervals not exceeding 10 years. It is not a certificate, it is a report, which should be used to identify any faults or potential faults within an installation that may have developed over a period of time. Where faults or potential faults are found, they must be recorded as observations; these observations are classified at three levels:

- Classification C1 indicates that the observation found was dangerous and should be dealt with immediately, as there is a risk of injury present.
- Classification C2 would be given where there was a potentially dangerous situation, which should be dealt with urgently. C2 could also be used where further investigation is required; in these instances, the investigation should be carried out as quickly as possible.
- Classification C3 is for observations that are not unsafe but improvements are recommended and should be considered.

Typical examples of classifications are:

- C1 would be where a live conductor or live part could be touched, perhaps where a protective device is missing and the space has not been covered with a blanking device.
- C2 would be where an incorrect rating of protective device has been installed. Further investigation required could be where there is no evidence of protective bonding.
- C3 is used where the installation does not comply with the latest edition of BS7671; for example, a domestic installation pre-2019 does not have rcd protection on lighting circuits, socket outlets or circuits used in a bathroom.

Where a classification of C1 or C2 has been issued, the installation must be given an overall assessment of unsatisfactory; classification of C3 would be given an assessment of satisfactory.

Where an electrical installation condition report has been issued, it must be accompanied by a schedule of inspections and a schedule of test results.

It is very important to note that an electrical installation condition report should only be undertaken by persons who are experienced in the type of installation being inspected. Inspecting and testing of existing installations is a very skilled job and requires a great deal of knowledge and understanding. For this reason, detailed explanation on this type of work is not included in this book.

ELECTRIC SHOCK

As stated right at the beginning of this book, electricity can be very dangerous if it is not treated with respect. Accidents can, and sometimes do, result in serious injury and even death.

Even the smallest electric shock can be fatal. Although it may not be a shock large enough to burn you, it may be large enough to cause a reflex action, which in turn could result in you falling from a pair of steps or a ladder. As an example: 1mA, which is 0.001 (1/1000) of an amp, is the current produced by an insulation resistance tester, which is regarded as the level that most people can feel as an electric shock. I suggest that if you have not already done so by accident, that you hold the probes of your insulation resistance test leads one in each hand and push the test button just to experience a shock of 1mA.

If the shock current rises to 10mA, most people will suffer muscular contraction and find it difficult, if not impossible, to let go of anything that is in their hand.

At 18mA, if the shock is across the chest, it will be impossible for most healthy people to breath and there is a strong possibility of burns

A shock current of between 50mA and 80mA will almost certainly result in ventricular fibrillation; in this situation CPR (cardiopulmonary resuscitation) is required to prevent death. Of course, all humans are different and the effects may change slightly for the given values. However, it is clear just how dangerous electricity can be and why we always need to take great care to ensure the safety of ourselves and others.

Megger.

ELECTRICAL INSTALLATION CONDITION REPORT

SECTION A. DETAILS OF THE PERSON ORDERING THE REPORT

Name

Address

SECTION B. REASON FOR PRODUCING THIS REPORT

Date(s) on which inspection and testing was carried out

SECTION C. DETAILS OF THE INSTALLATION WHICH IS THE SUBJECT OF THIS REPORT

Occupier

Address

Description of premises

Domestic ☐   Commercial ☐   Industrial ☐   Other (include brief description) ☐

Estimated age of wiring system   years

Evidence of additions / alterations   Yes ☐   No ☐   Not apparent ☐   If yes, estimate age   years

Installation records available? (Regulation 651.1)   Yes ☐   No ☐   Date of last inspection   (date)

SECTION D. EXTENT AND LIMITATIONS OF INSPECTION AND TESTING

Extent of the electrical installation covered by this report

Agreed limitations including the reasons (see Regulation 653.2)

Agreed with:

Operational limitations including the reasons (see page no   )

The inspection and testing detailed in this report and accompanying schedules have been carried out in accordance with BS 7671:2018 (IET Wiring Regulations) as amended to

It should be noted that cables concealed within trunking and conduits, under floors, in roof spaces, and generally within the fabric of the building or underground, have **not** been inspected unless specifically agreed between the client and inspector prior to the inspection. An inspection should be made within an accessible roof space housing other electrical equipment.

SECTION E. SUMMARY OF THE CONDITION OF THE INSTALLATION

General condition of the installation (in terms of electrical safety)

Overall assessment of the installation in terms of its suitability for continued use

*An unsatisfactory assessment indicates that dangerous (code C1) and/or potentially dangerous (code C2) conditions have been identified

SECTION F. RECOMMENDATIONS

Where the overall assessment of the suitability of the installation for continued use above is stated as UNSATISFACTORY, I/We recommend that any observations classified as 'Danger present' (code C1) or 'Potentially dangerous' (code C2) are acted upon as a matter of urgency.   Investigation without delay is recommended for observations identified as 'Further investigation required' (code FI). Observations classified as 'Improvement recommended' (code C3) should be given due consideration.

Subject to the necessary remedial action being taken, I/We recommend that the installation is further inspected and tested by

SECTION G. DECLARATION

I/We, being the person(s) responsible for the inspection and testing of the electrical installation (as indicated by my/our signatures below), particulars of which are described above, having exercised reasonable skill and care when carrying out the inspection and testing, hereby declare that the information in this report, including the observations and the attached schedules, provides an accurate assessment of the condition of the electrical installation taking into account the stated extent and limitations in section D of this report.

Inspected and tested by:	Report authorised for issue by:
Name (Capitals)	Name (Capitals)
Signature	Signature
For/on behalf of	For/on behalf of
Position	Position
Address	Address
Date	Date

SECTION H. SCHEDULE(S)

          schedule(s) of inspection and   schedule(s) of test results are attached.

The attached schedule(s) are part of this document and this report is valid only when they are attached to it.

This form was developed by Megger Limited and is based on the model shown in Appendix 6 of BS7671:2018 © Megger Limited 2018

Electrical installation condition report (continued opposite).

Certificate No: 1

SECTION I. SUPPLY CHARACTERISTICS AND EARTHING ARRANGEMENTS

Earthing arrangements	Number and Type of Live Conductors		Nature of supply Parameters		Supply Protective Device
TN-C	AC	DC	Nominal voltage, U/U_0 (1)	V	BS (EN)
TN-S	1-phase, 2-wire	2-wire	Nominal frequency, f (1)	Hz	
TN-C-S	2-phase, 3-wire	3-wire	Prospective fault current I_{pf} (2)	kA	Type
TT	3-phase, 3-wire	Other	External loop impedance, Z_e (2)	Ω	
IT	3-phase, 4-wire		Note: (1) by enquiry		Rated current A
	Confirmation of supply polarity		(2) by enquiry or by measurement		

Other sources of supply (as detailed on attached schedule)

SECTION J. PARTICULARS OF INSTALLATION REFERRED TO IN THE REPORT

Means of Earthing

Details of Installation Earth Electrode *(where applicable)*

Distributor's facility	Type
Installation earth electrode	Location
	Resistance to Earth Ω

Main Protective Conductors

Earthing conductor	Material	csa	mm²	Connection / continuity verified
Main protective bonding conductors (to extraneous-conductive-parts)	Material	csa	mm²	Connection / continuity verified

To water installation pipes	To gas installation pipes	To oil installation pipes	To structural steel
To lightning protection	To other	Specify	

Main Switch / Switch-Fuse / Circuit-Breaker / RCD

Location	Current rating A	**If RCD main switch**	
BS(EN)	Fuse / device rating or setting A	Rated residual operating current ($I_{\Delta n}$)	mA
No of poles	Voltage rating V	Rated time delay	ms
		Measured operating time	ms

SECTION K. OBSERVATIONS

Referring to the attached schedules of inspection and test results, and subject to the limitations specified at the *Extent and limitations of inspection* and testing section.

No remedial action is required   The following observations are made   (see below)

OBSERVATION(S) Include schedule reference, as appropriate	CLASSIFICATION CODE

One of the following codes, as appropriate, has been allocated to each of the observations made above to indicate to the person(s) responsible for the installation the degree of urgency for remedial action.

C1 - Danger present. Risk of injury. Immediate remedial action required
C2 - Potentially dangerous - urgent remedial action required
C3 - Improvement recommended
FI - Further investigation required without delay

Page 2 of 6

This form was developed by Megger Limited and is based on the model shown in Appendix 6 of BS7671: 2018   © Megger Limited 2018

Electrical installation condition report (continued overleaf).

CONDITION REPORT INSPECTION SCHEDULE FOR
DOMESTIC AND SIMILAR PREMISES WITH UP TO 100 A SUPPLY

Certificate No: 1

Note: This form is suitable for many types of smaller installation not exclusively domestic.

OUTCOMES	Acceptable condition	✓	Unacceptable condition	State C1 or C2	Improvement recommended	State C3	Further investigation	FI	Not verified	N/V	Limitation	LIM	Not applicable	N/A

ITEM NO	DESCRIPTION	OUTCOME (Use codes above. Provide additional comment where appropriate C1, C2, C3 and FI coded items to be recorded in Section K of the Condition Report)	
1.0	EXTERNAL CONDITION OF INTAKE EQUIPMENT (VISUAL INSPECTION ONLY)		
1.1	Service cable		
1.2	Service head		
1.3	Earthing arrangement		
1.4	Meter tails		
1.5	Metering equipment		
1.6	Isolator (where present)		
2.0	PRESENCE OF ADEQUATE ARRANGEMENTS FOR OTHER SOURCES SUCH AS MICROGENERATORS (551.6; 551.7)		
3.0	EARTHING / BONDING ARRANGEMENTS (411.3; Chap 54)		
3.1	Presence and condition of distributor's earthing arrangements (542.1.2.1; 542.1.2.2)		
3.2	Presence and condition of earth electrode connection where applicable (542.1.2.3)		
3.3	Provision of earthing / bonding labels at all appropriate locations (514.13.1)		
3.4	Confirmation of earthing conductor size (542.3; 543.1.1)		
3.5	Accessibility and condition of earthing conductor at MET (543.3.2)		
3.6	Confirmation of main protective bonding conductor sizes (544.1)		
3.7	Condition and accessibility of main protective bonding conductor connections (543.3.2; 544.1.2)		
3.8	Accessibility and condition of other protective bonding connections (543.3.1; 543.3.2)		
4.0	COMSUMER UNIT(S) / DISTRIBUTION BOARD(S)		
4.1	Adequacy of working space / accessibility to consumer unit / distribution board (132.12; 513.1)		
4.2	Security of fixing (134.1.1)		
4.3	Condition of enclosure(s) in terms of IP rating etc (416.2)		
4.4	Condition of enclosure(s) in terms of fire rating etc (421.1.201; 526.5)		
4.5	Enclosure not damaged/deteriorated so as to impair safety (651.2)		
4.6	Presence of main linked switch (as required by 462.1.201)		
4.7	Operation of main switch (functional check) (643.10)		
4.8	Manual operation of circuit-breakers and RCDs to prove disconnection (643.10)		
4.9	Correct identification of circuit details and protective devices (514.8.1; 514.9.1)		
4.10	Presence of RCD six-monthly test notice at or near consumer unit / distribution board (514.12.2)		
4.11	Presence of non-standard (mixed) cable colour warning notice at or near consumer unit / distribution board (514.14)		
4.12	Presence of alternative supply warning notice at or near consumer unit / distribution board (514.15)		
4.13	Presence of other required labelling (please specify) (Section 514)		
4.14	Compatibility of protective devices, bases and other components; correct type and rating (No signs of unacceptable thermal damage, arcing or overheating) (411.3.2; 411.4; 411.5; 411.6; Sections 432, 433)		
4.15	Single-pole switching or protective devices in line conductor only (132.14.1; 530.3.3)		
4.16	Protection against mechanical damage where cables enter consumer unit / distribution board (132.14.1; 522.8.1; 522.8.5; 522.8.11)		
4.17	Protection against electromagnetic effects where cables enter consumer unit / distribution board / enclosures (521.5.1)		
4.18	RCD(s) provided for fault protection - includes RCBOs (411.4.204; 411.5.2; 531.2)		
4.19	RCD(s) provided for additional protection - includes RCBOs (411.3.3; 415.1)		
4.20	Confirmation of indication that SPD is functional (651.4)		
4.21	Confirmation that ALL conductor connections, including connections to busbars are correctly located in terminals and are tight and secure (526.1)		
4.22	Adequate arrangements where a generating set operates as a switched alternative to the public supply (551.6)		
4.23	Adequate arrangements where a generating set operates in parallel with the public supply (551.7)		

This form was developed by Megger Limited and is based on the model shown in Appendix 6 of BS7671: 2018 © Megger Limited 2018

Page 4 of 6

Electrical installation condition report (continued opposite).

Certificate No: 1

OUTCOMES	Acceptable condition	✓	Unacceptable condition	State C1 or C2	Improvement recommended	State C3	Further Investigation	FI	Not verified	N/V	Limitation	LIM	Not applicable	N/A

ITEM NO	DESCRIPTION	OUTCOME (Use codes above. Provide additional comment where appropriate C1, C2, C3 and FI coded items to be recorded in Section K of the Condition Report)	
5.0	**FINAL CIRCUITS**		
5.1	Identification of conductors (514.3.1)		
5.2	Cables correctly supported throughout their run (521.10.202; 522.8.5)		
5.3	Condition of insulation of live parts (416.1)		
5.4	Non-sheathed cables protected by enclosure in conduit, ducting or trunking (521.10.1)		
	To include the integrity of conduit and trunking systems (metallic and plastic)		
5.5	Adequacy of cables for current-carrying capacity with regard for the type and nature of installation (Section 523)		
5.6	Coordination between conductors and overload protective devices (433.1; 533.2.1)		
5.7	Adequacy of protective devices: type and rated current for fault protection (411.3)		
5.8	Presence and adequacy of circuit protective conductors (411.3.1; Section 543)		
5.9	Wiring system(s) appropriate for the type and nature of the installation and external influences (Section 522)		
5.10	Concealed cables installed in prescribed zones (See section D. Extent and Limitations) (522.6.202)		
5.11	Cables concealed under floors, above ceilings or in walls/partitions, adequately protected against damage (see Section D. Extent and limitations) (522.6.204)		
5.12	Provision of additional protection by RCD not exceeding 30 mA:		
	for all socket-outlets of rating 32 A or less, unless an exception is permitted (411.3.3)		
	for the supply of mobile equipment not exceeding 32 A rating for use outdoors (411.3.3)		
	for cables concealed in walls at a depth of less than 50 mm (522.6.202; 522.6.203)		
	for cables concealed in walls / partitions containing metal parts regardless of depth (522.6.203)		
	Final circuits supplying luminaires within domestic (household) premises (411.3.4)		
5.13	Provision of fire barriers, sealing arrangements and protection against thermal effects (Section 527)		
5.14	Band II cables segregated / separated from Band I cables (528.1)		
5.15	Cables segregated / separated from communications cabling (528.2)		
5.16	Cables segregated / separated from non-electrical services (528.3)		
5.17	Termination of cables at enclosures - indicated extent of sampling in Section D of the report (Section 526)		
	Connections soundly made and under no undue strain (526.6)		
	No basic insulation of a conductor visible outside enclosure (526.8)		
	Connections of live conductors adequately enclosed (526.5)		
	Adequately connected at point of entry to enclosure (glands, bushes etc.) (522.8.5)		
5.18	Condition of accessories including socket-outlets, switches and joint boxes (651.2(v))		
5.19	Suitability of accessories for external influences (512.2)		
5.20	Adequacy of working space / accessibility to equipment (132.12; 513.1)		
5.21	Single-pole switching or protective devices in line conductors only (132.14.1, 530.3.3)		
6.0	**LOCATION(S) CONTAINING A BATH OR SHOWER**		
6.1	Additional protection for all low voltage (LV) circuits by RCD not exceeding 30 mA (701.411.3.3)		
6.2	Where used as a protective measure, requirements for SELV or PELV met (701.414.4.5)		
6.3	Shaver sockets comply with BS EN 61558-2-5 formerly BS 3535 (701.512.3)		
6.4	Presence of supplementary bonding conductors, unless not required by BS 7671:2018 (701.415.2)		
6.5	Low voltage (e.g. 230 volt) socket-outlets sited at least 3 m from zone 1 (701.512.3)		
6.6	Suitability of equipment for external influences for installed location in terms of IP rating (701.512.2)		
6.7	Suitability of accessories and controlgear etc. for a particular zone (701.512.3)		
6.8	Suitability of current-using equipment for particular position within the location (701.55)		
7.0	**OTHER PART 7 SPECIAL INSTALLATIONS OR LOCATIONS**		
7.1	List all other special installations or locations present, if any. (Record separately the results of particular inspections applied.)		

Inspected by:
Name (Capitals) Signature Date Page 5 of 6

This form was developed by Megger Limited and is based on the model shown
in Appendix 6 of BS7671: 2018 © Megger Limited 2018

Electrical installation condition report (continued overleaf).

GENERIC SCHEDULE OF TEST RESULTS

Certificate No: 1

DB reference no
Location
Zs at DB Ω
I$_{pf}$ at DB (kA)
Correct supply polarity confirmed
Phase sequence confirmed (where appropriate)

Details of circuits and/or installed equipment vulnerable to damage when testing

Details of test instruments used (state serial and/or asset numbers)
Continuity
Insulation resistance
Earth fault loop impedance
RCD
Earth electrode resistance

Tested by:
Name (Capitals)
Signature
Date

		Circuit Details															Test results									
			Protective device					Conductor details			Ring final circuit continuity Ω			Continuity Ω (R1 + R2) or R2		Insulation Resistance (MΩ)			Polarity	Maximum measured Zs Ω	RCD		AFDD		Remarks (continue on a seperate sheet if necessary)
Circuit number	Circuit Description	BS (EN)	Type	rating (A)	breaking capacity (kA)	RCD I Δn (mA)	Maximum permitted Zs (Ω*)	Reference Method	Live (mm2)	cpc (mm2)	r1 (line)	rn (neutral)	r2 (cpc)	(R1 + R2)	R2	Test Voltage V	Live - Live	Live - Earth			Disconnection time (ms)	RCD test button operation	Manual AFDD test	AFDD button operation	
1	2	3	4	5	6	7	8	9	10	11	12	13	14	15	16	17	18	19	20	21	22	23	24	25	

* Where the maximum permitted earth fault loop impedance value stated in column 8 is taken from a source other than the tabulated values given in Chapter 41 of this Standard, state the source of the data in the appropriate cell for the circuit in the 'Remarks' column (column 25) of the schedule.

Electrical installation condition report (continued).

CHAPTER 2

Working Safely

SAFE ISOLATION

While it is true that some of the tests that we carry out on electrical installations are live tests, these tests are carried out using the correct equipment. Procedures are in place that must be followed to ensure that the person carrying out the testing, and any other persons, remain safe. We must never attempt to work on electrical equipment while it is still live.

To be safe we must take all of the precautions possible because, as we know, you cannot see electricity and usually, unless something is going wrong, you cannot smell or hear it. The best way to ensure safety when carrying out electrical work is to isolate the installation or the circuit that is being worked on. There is a well-documented procedure in place for this, which, believe it or not, is called the Safe Isolation Procedure and, providing we carry it out properly every time we need to isolate a circuit, we will be safe. When working on electrical systems, unless you are very sure it is safe to do so, never take short-cuts and never rush safe isolation.

The Electricity at Work Regulations

These state that:

No person shall be engaged in any work activity on or so near any live conductor (*other than one suitably covered with insulating material so as to prevent danger*) that danger may arise unless:

- It is unreasonable in all the circumstances for it to be dead; and
- It is reasonable in all the circumstances for him to be at work on or near it while it is live; and
- Suitable precautions (including where necessary the provision of suitable protective equipment) are taken to prevent injury.

As the EAWR 1989 is a statutory document, this means that anyone working on an electrical installation who is not complying with the requirements of it may be breaking the law.

Voltage indicator, padlock and notice.

The equipment we need is an approved voltage isolator or test lamp, a padlock and a notice.

Safe Isolation Procedure

- Ensure that the circuit that is to be isolated is live, do not take a chance and assume it is live. We need to make sure that we are the ones who are isolating it; if we do not prove it is live to start with, it could be that we isolate the wrong circuit, and that the one we are working on gets switched on and becomes live while we are working on it. This can be done by just turning on the circuit and seeing if it works, or an approved test lamp or voltage indicator can be used. Do not use any piece of test equipment that has a switch on it, as if it is on the wrong setting or switched off, it may indicate that it is not live when in fact it is.
- Trace the point of isolation, which could be a type of switch, a circuit breaker or a fuse.
- Turn off the switch or circuit breaker and use a locking off device to ensure that it cannot be turned back on until you want it to be.
- Attach a notice at the point of isolation to indicate to others that the circuit has been isolated for a reason.
- Check that the circuit to be worked on is dead, using your approved voltage indicator.
- If the circuit looks like it is dead, check that the voltage indicator is working by testing it on a known supply or by using a proving unit.
- Recheck the circuit to be worked on.
- If it is dead, then it is safe to start work.

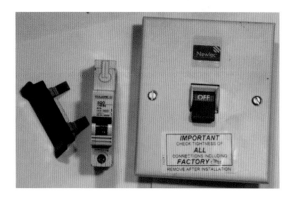

Isolator, fuse and circuit breaker.

Safe Isolation Flowchart

Check that the circuit is live.

⬇

Identify the point of isolation.

⬇

Isolate and lock off.

⬇

Fix notice by the point of isolation.

⬇

Use a voltage indicator/test lamp to check that the circuit is dead.

⬇

Prove that the voltage indicator/test lamp is functioning correctly by checking it on a known supply or proving unit.

⬇

Recheck that the circuit is dead and if it is, then it is safe to commence work.

MANUAL HANDLING

Of all injuries that last over 3 days and are reported to the Health and Safety Executive, 38 per cent are caused by manual handling.

Wherever possible it is best to avoid lifting/moving heavy loads, but of course it is not always possible, as even trying to gain access to lift a floorboard may require the moving of a piece of heavy furniture. If something needs to be moved or lifted, it is wise to take a few moments to assess the situation and perhaps decide on recruiting some help or even, in some cases, a mechanical lifting aid.

On the occasions when lifting is unavoidable, there are a few simple precautions that can be taken to reduce the risk of injury:

- Think before lifting, and plan the lift.
- Can handling aids be used?
- Where is the load going to be placed?
- Will help be required with the load?
- Ensure that, if possible, you are facing in the direction that you will move having lifted the object.
- Make sure that all obstructions have been moved.
- Consider stopping and resting the load on a surface at intervals along the route as this will enable you to change your grip.

Correct lifting position.

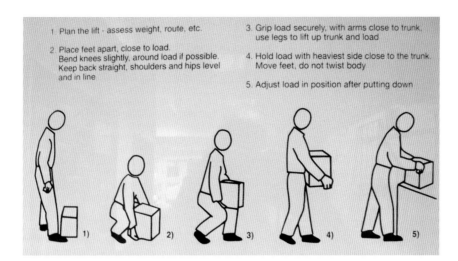

1. Plan the lift - assess weight, route, etc.

2. Place feet apart, close to load. Bend knees slightly, around load if possible. Keep back straight, shoulders and hips level and in line.

3. Grip load securely, with arms close to trunk, use legs to lift up trunk and load

4. Hold load with heaviest side close to the trunk. Move feet, do not twist body

5. Adjust load in position after putting down

- Ensure that you are able to put the object down onto a suitable level surface on completion of the lift.

When lifting:

- Adopt a stable position before attempting to lift.
- Make sure that you can get a good hold on the object before attempting to lift it.
- Keep the load close to the body.
- Lift keeping your back straight, if possible.
- Avoid twisting or flexing your back.
- Move smoothly and keep your head up when handling.
- If your grip feels uncomfortable, put the load down and start again.

WORKING AT HEIGHT

Most of us at some point will need to work on, or install, equipment which is too high to reach from the ground without using some form of access equipment. On these occasions it is important that we work safely. In 2008/2009 over 4,000 major injuries were caused from falls at height.

It is important when working that we use the correct type of tools, including access equipment. Of course, there are many types of equipment that we can use if we are working at height. These can range from a simple hop-up for lower levels, right through to a full scaffold for major work at heights.

Providing we follow a few simple rules and use equipment that is suitable for the job, we will remain safe.

Step-Ladders

When working off step-ladders, always ensure that you are working from a level surface. We can, of course, ensure that the ladder is upright by using packing under the step-ladder feet; if we do, we must always make sure that the packing is secure and that the feet of the ladder cannot slip off.

- Before use, always check them for safety; this includes looking at the feet.
- Ensure that they are fully open before attempting to climb them.
- Ensure that any locking devices are used.
- Never work off the top two steps.
- Never overreach.
- Avoid working side-on; always try and face the item you are working on.
- Try not to work from steps for more than 30 minutes without a break.
- Do not use steps if working with loads greater than 10kg.
- Never ever work on anything if you feel unsafe – always trust your instincts; if it feels unsafe, it is unsafe.

Step-ladder correctly positioned.

Ladders

When it comes to working from ladders, always ensure that the ground is firm and level.

* Before use, always check the ladder for damage/wear and tear.
* Make sure that you have a good resting point for the top of the ladder; never rest it against the guttering or down pipes.
* Never work from a ladder for more than 30 minutes without a break.
* When setting the ladder, it should be at an angle of 75 degrees; this works out at a ratio of 1:4 (the foot of the ladder must be 1 unit out for every 4 units up).
* Wherever possible, get somebody to foot the ladder (stand on the bottom).
* When climbing the ladder. always make sure that both hands are free to hold onto the ladder stiles.
* Never hold on to the ladder rungs when climbing the ladder.
* Never work off the top three steps.
* Never overreach.
* Always secure the ladder before working from it.
* Never lean back off a ladder; use a piece of equipment called an easy reach to lift the ladder from the wall.

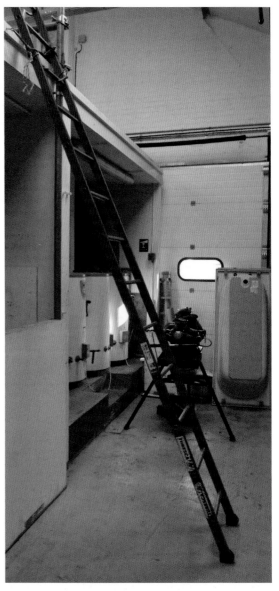

Ladder correctly positioned.

Remember! If it feels unsafe, it is unsafe.

Tower Scaffold

Whenever you are working from a tower, always make sure that it is erected to comply with the manufacturers' instructions. The feet, braces, and outriggers are there for a purpose and should always be used.

Tower scaffold.

- Make sure that the area where the tower is to be erected is level and firm.
- Never climb up the outside of a tower scaffold.
- Never use steps or a ladder off a tower scaffold.
- Never overreach.

Some electrical jobs will require the erection of a free-standing scaffold. This type of scaffold should always be erected by a professional scaffolder, and on completion must have a label fixed to it to show that it has been erected correctly and is safe. This is know as a 'scaff tag'. The scaffold should be checked and the tag updated at regular intervals – often this will be weekly.

Scaffold safety tag.

CHAPTER 3

Tools and Equipment

To carry out electrical work safely and correctly you almost have to be a general builder. Very often the connection of the cables and electrical accessories is the easiest part of the job. Finding a route for, and installing, the cables is often the most difficult.

Having the correct tools for a job and knowing how to use them correctly can save a lot of time and make the job so much easier.

A basic electrician's kit must consist of:

• A claw hammer for fixing cable clips, helping to lift floorboards and various other tasks.
• A club hammer for heavy work, such as chasing walls.
• A pair of electrician's pliers to use for preparing the cable conductors for termination.
• A pair of side-cutters to cut cable with.
• Cable insulation stripper to strip off the cable insulation, as required.
• Gland nut pliers, also called pump pliers.
• Small, terminal screwdriver.
• Medium and large, flat-end screwdriver.
• Small, medium and large Phillips (cross-head) screwdriver.
• Tape measure.
• A set of wood drill bits.
• A set of metal drill bits.
• Selection of masonry drills.
• A wood brace.
• A hand drill (wheel brace).
• Wood saw.
• Junior hacksaw.

• A hacksaw.
• Pad saw for cutting holes in plasterboard.
• A brick bolster for using to chase brick and plaster walls.
• A floor bolster to help lift floorboards (very often an electrician will use this as a brick bolster as well).
• A selection of cold chisels.
• A knife for stripping cables.
• A knife with a retractable blade for cutting plasterboard and other materials. (This type of knife is not particularly suitable for stripping cables, although some electricians use them.)
• A small spirit-level for use when fitting accessories.
• A large spirit-level when setting out.
• A set of wood chisels.
• Small trowel.

Tools to Make Life Easier

An electric power drill, either a battery or a low-voltage drill. A battery drill is preferable in many instances, as it eliminates the need to have the power switched on. It is advisable to keep a spare battery, which is fully charged, as you will find that the battery always runs flat at the most inconvenient time. You will need to ensure that the drill is powerful enough to carry out the work expected of it. If it is to be used for drilling holes in walls for screw fixings, you will need a percussion drill. It is also very important to remember that, if you overload your drill, it will burn out. Always try to keep pressure on the drill bit – it will last longer.

SDS drill and chuck.

Most modern battery drills have a variable speed; it is very convenient to adapt this type of drill for use as an electric screwdriver, although it is advisable not to use it when fixing to a surface accessories such as Bakelite boxes or ceiling roses. This is because it is too easy for you to accidentally over-tighten the fixing screws and break the accessory; it can prove to be an expensive lesson.

It is important also to ensure that the type of drill bits you buy are suitable for use with the type of drill you have. Most modern drills come with an SDS (special direct system) chuck and the drill bits simply push in and are held secure by a mechanism inside the drill. This type of chuck eliminates the use of a key to tighten the chuck onto the drill bit.

Head torch.

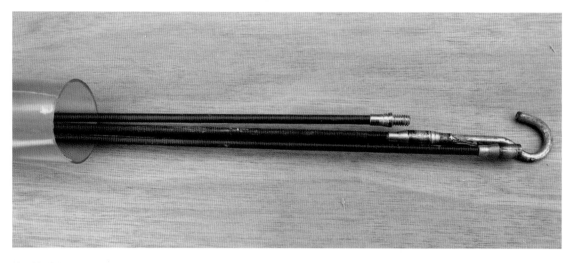

Flexible fishing tool.

Another useful point is that a key chuck can be used as they are available with an SDS-type fitting, which fits into the end of the drill just as a drill bit would. This, of course, makes an SDS drill very versatile and resolves the problem of trying to find the chuck key, which you have put down somewhere but cannot remember where; also, the drill bit always remains tight in the chuck.

Other useful tools include:

- A small circular saw to cut through flooring.
- A torch for working in dark areas, possibly a head lamp to leave your hands free.
- A small, hand-held mirror for looking in confined spaces, such as under floors.
- A flexible rod for fishing under floors.
- A small bucket for holding plaster/sand and cement, which is used for making good chases around boxes.

CHAPTER 4

Voltage Bands

VOLTAGE BANDS

Electrical supplies to installations that we will be working on are known as low-voltage supplies and are 230V for a single-phase supply and 400V for a three-phase supply.

The electrical energy that we use is supplied to us through the National Grid system. At various places around the country there are power stations that generate our electricity using many types of fuel to drive the generator turbines. These produce electricity at 25,000V (25kV). Once the energy has been generated, it must be transmitted over the country to wherever it is required. The system used is known as the National Grid. Our grid system operates at a voltages of 275,000V (275kV) and 400,000V (400kV). The high voltages are used to reduce power losses and these voltages are obtained by using step-up transformers at the point of generation. When our electricity gets close to the point where it is going to be used, it enters a substation where the voltage is reduced to either 33,000V (33kV) or 11,000V (11kV). From the substation it is distributed to local transformers, which you can see dotted around cities, towns and villages.

From these local transformers, the supply is delivered into our building, ready for use. These supply voltages will be either 230V for a single-phase supply or 400V for a three-phase supply.

Our supply voltage is described as being low voltage and this is the term used to describe any voltage of between 50V a.c. and 1,000V a.c., and 120V d.c up to 1,500V d.c.

Voltages of less than low voltage are described as extra-low voltage; this term is used for voltages of 0V d.c. up to 120V d.c., and 0V a.c. up to 50V a.c. Voltages of above low voltage are described as high voltage and are rarely used in our installations.

In a normal electrical installation we usually have equipment that operates at either extra-low voltage or low voltage, and to simplify matters, the circuits that supply this equipment are referred to

Supply transformer.

as band 1 and band 2 circuits. Band 1 is for circuits that supply equipment at extra-low voltage – these would include most alarm systems, telecommunication systems, and so on. Band 2 is for circuits that supply equipment that operates at low voltage – these circuits would include our lighting and power circuits, which are installed in most dwellings.

EXTRA-LOW VOLTAGE

Although extra-low voltage is any voltage between 0V and 120V d.c. and 0V and 50V a.c., we have different types of extra-low voltage, which are referred to as SELV, PELV and FELV.

At this point we can forget about d.c. voltages, as most types of d.c. circuits are supplied by battery circuits or transformers.

SELV

This stands for Separated Extra-Low Voltage. This type of circuit is supplied through an isolating transformer, which reduces the voltage from low voltage on the primary side of the transformer down to any voltage of up to 50V on the secondary side. The reason that it is called separated is that the wiring on the secondary side of the transformer has no contact at all with the wiring on the primary side; this includes the earthing system. The isolating transformer also has to be manufactured to the required standard, which is BS EN 61558-2-6.

A typical SELV circuit would be an extra-low voltage circuit used for lighting. These are often sup-plied by individual transformers for each luminaire or possibly one transformer may supply a number of luminaires. SELV circuits can also be used to provide protection from electric shock in bathrooms, although there are further restrictions on voltages, usually as low as 12V.

PELV

PELV is the term used for a Protected Extra-Low Voltage circuit. This type of circuit would be supplied through an isolating transformer, just as a SELV circuit would be. The difference is that the circuit would also be provided with an earthing system, which is common to both low and extra-low voltage.

FELV

Functional Extra-Low Voltage is similar in many ways to both SELV and PELV, the main difference being that a FELV transformer will not meet the strict requirements set out for the transformers used for SELV and FELV, and for that reason cannot be used in the same environments.

REDUCED LOW VOLTAGE

This is a term used to describe a voltage of 55V to earth or 110V between live conductors. Most of us will know that 110V transformers are commonly used to supply hand-held tools, which are often used on construction sites. Most electric shocks are received due to a fault that makes metalwork in an area live; when using hand tools, the live met-

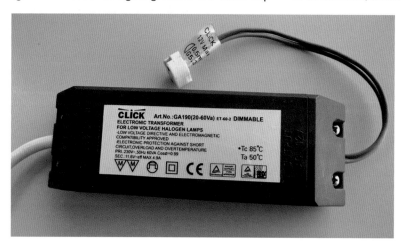

SELV transformer.

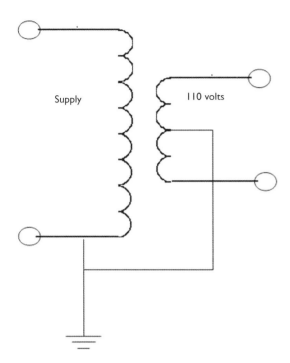

110V centre tapped transformer.

Typical keyway socket.

alwork could be the case of the tool being used. Although the tools operate using a voltage of 110V, the maximum shock voltage to earth is limited by the use of a centre tapped transformer.

Although it is accepted that most of our socket outlets are low voltage at 230V, and are identified by the use of our rectangular-shaped plugs and sockets, it is not unusual for industrial plug and socket outlets to BS EN 60309 to be used. The outlets for different types of voltages are usually identified by the use of colours; this is because the physical size of the outlets is the same for each current rating and does not alter for the different voltages

A key system is used to prevent a plug of one voltage rating from being plugged into a socket with a different voltage rating. If you look at any industrial plug or socket, you will see that the plug has a small plastic projection and the socket has a keyway; this ensures that the correct combination is always used, as the earth pin for each voltage is placed at varying positions relating to a clock face around the plug and socket in relation to the keyway. If you look at a BS EN 60309 110V plug end-on and position the keyway at the bottom, you will see that the earth pin (largest) is at a position of 4 o'clock. This type of plug is known as a 4h. All of the other types of low-voltage plugs can be identified in the same way. For instance, a 230V 2-pin and earth plug will have its earth pin at 6 o'clock at the bottom of the plug and is a 6h.

Extra-low voltage plug and sockets use a different type of system, which is called a major keyway system. The violet 25V plugs have a keyway at the bottom, the 50V plugs have a keyway at the top and bottom, and the d.c. plugs have offset keyways.

Identifying voltages by colour.

Voltage Range	Frequency Range	Colour Code
20–25 V	50/60Hz	Purple
40–50 V	50/60Hz	White
100–130 V	50/60Hz	Yellow
200–250 V	50/60Hz	Blue
380–480 V	50/60Hz	Red
500–690 V	50/60Hz	Black
—	>60–500Hz	Green
None of the above		Grey

CHAPTER 5

Dealing with Cables

Because electrical systems are used in many different types of environment, it is necessary to have different types of cables and installation methods, which are suitable for use in the environment in which they are to be installed.

TYPES OF CABLES

Before we can consider installing cables it is important to know which types of cables are suitable for various types of installations. We must also make sure that we select a cable with the correct current rating.

To ensure that the cables that we use can be selected correctly, they are manufactured to standard sizes using a particular quality of copper for the conductors. For this reason, it is very important that only cables manufactured to British Standards are used; this will ensure that, once the correct size

and current rating of the cable has been chosen, it will be safe to install.

Cables are sized in mm^2; in other words the size of the cable is chosen by the cross-sectional area of the conductor, not by its diameter. A conductor can be made up of one strand of copper or it can be many strands twisted together to make up the required size.

The smallest size that we can use for a low-voltage fixed installation is $1mm^2$ and usually the largest size that would be used in a domestic installation would be $25mm^2$.

FLAT MULTICORE AND EARTH CABLE

The most common type of cable used domestically for fixed wiring is flat thermoplastic PVC 70°C multicore and earth cable with copper conductors;

Common sizes of twin and earth cable.

CSA of live conductors	CSA of circuit protective conductor	Type of conductors
$1mm^2$	$1mm^2$	Solid
$1.5mm^2$	$1mm^2$	Solid
$2.5mm^2$	$1.5mm^2$	Solid
$4mm^2$	$1.5mm^2$	Stranded live conductors solid CPC
$6mm^2$	$2.5mm^2$	Stranded live conductors solid CPC
$10mm^2$	$4mm^2$	Stranded
$16mm^2$	$6mm^2$	Stranded
$25mm^2$	$10mm^2$	Stranded

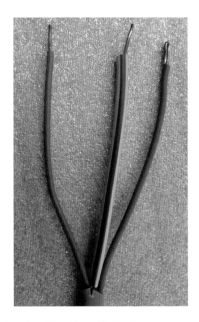

Twin and earth cable with earth sleeving.

Three-core and earth cable.

this type of cable is intended to operate at temperatures of up to 70°C. This does not mean that the cable can be installed in temperatures of 70°C. The temperature represents the maximum temperature at which the copper conductor can operate without causing damage to the cable insulation.

The cable has insulated live conductors with the protective earthing conductor being left bare. At the points where this conductor is terminated to accessories, it must be covered using a purpose-made green and yellow sleeve. It is very easy to install and can be clipped directly to surfaces, passed through building voids, plastered into walls or contained in trunking or conduit. The method of installation will depend on the type of environment and building construction.

Twin and earth cables are manufactured in standard sizes with two or three live conductors; the live conductors are insulated and the earth (CPC) is usually left bare. The cables are commonly referred to as twin and earth or three core and earth.

The cable can be terminated by stripping back the outer sheath, which is its mechanical protection. This can be done using a knife, although great care must be taken to ensure that you do not cut through the conductor insulation.

Another method is to expose the CPC and pull it outwards; this will tear through the mechanical protection.

Once enough of the insulated conductors have been exposed, the mechanical protection can be removed by cutting it off with a knife or by using side-cutters.

PVC cable being stripped with knife.

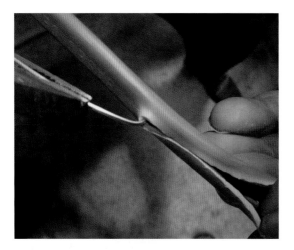

PVC being stripped by pulling CPC.

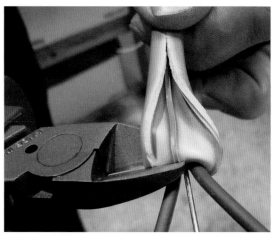

Mechanical protection cut-off.

Now that the insulated conductors are exposed, the ends need to be removed to allow the copper conductors to be terminated. Again, this can be removed by using a sharp knife or cable strippers. Never twist conductors together as this could result in a poor termination; the copper will also become work hardened and could possibly snap if ever they need to be disconnected.

Always ensure that about 5mm of mechanical protection remains inside the enclosure. The coloured insulation should never be visible outside of any enclosure.

If the conductor is to be connected into a terminal with no other conductors, the conductor should be bent double. This will require the insulation to be stripped back approximately 15mm. Where the cable is to be inserted into a terminal with other cables, then it should not be doubled over but just slipped in beside the other conductors. This, of course, will not require as much insulation to be removed.

Never attempt to remove the insulation by using side-cutters or pliers, as this may result in a small indent being made in the cable, which will be

Insulation removed using a cable stripper.

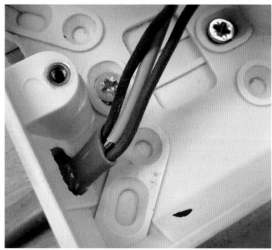

Mechanical protection removed.

Conductor bent double for connection.

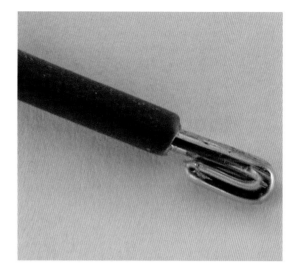

BELOW: *Conductor entered with other conductors.*

a weak spot. This could result in the cable fracturing when the accessory to which the cable has been terminated is pushed back to be fixed to its box.

STEEL WIRE ARMOUR CABLE

Steel wire armour cable is generally used where the cable may be exposed to harsh environments; in particular, where it is going to be buried or clipped

directly to a surface and may be exposed to impact. The cable can have as many cores as is practical and they are all the same CSA. All of the conductors are stranded and the size begins at $1.5mm^2$.

Beneath the PVC outer sheath of the cable there is a layer of steel wires, which are wrapped around the cable for its entire length. This provides a very strong protection against impact and it can also be used as a protective earthing conductor, if required. The use of the SWA for the earthing conductor will reduce the number of cable cores required; this in turn will make the cable slightly less expensive.

SWA cable can be installed using all of the same methods as PVC twin and earth, although if buried directly into a wall, the steel wire armour provides its own mechanical protection; of course, this type of cable is not as flexible as flat twin and earth.

Termination of an SWA cable requires the use of a special type of gland; these glands are available for use either outdoors or indoors. The outdoor type have a watertight seal and are a little more expensive.

It is important that SWA cables are terminated correctly because the glands used provide a means of earthing for the cable. It is very important that the SWA is earthed; even if it is not going to be used for the circuit earth, it will provide protection against electric shock if anyone accidently cuts through the cable.

Armoured cable glands.

Steel-wired armour cable.

The tools required for carrying out the termination of the gland are:

- Junior hacksaw.
- Large hacksaw with a blade that has 24 teeth per inch or more.
- Knife (but not a good idea to use a modelling knife as the blades are very sharp).
- Two pairs of gland nut pliers or two spanners.
- Pliers.

Step 1

Cut the cable to the required length using the large hacksaw. Be sure to allow enough for the cable termination. It is better to allow more than is required,

as you can always cut more off if necessary but it is very difficult to add bits on.

Step 2

Mark on the cable the point at which the gland is going to enter the enclosure. On this mark, wrap a piece of insulating tape around the cable. This will ensure that when you cut round the cable, the cut is straight.

Step 3

Cut the end of the gland shroud to fit the cable and put this onto the cable, then put the compression nut onto the cable. This may be difficult after stripping the cable.

RIGHT: *SWA cable marked using tape.*

BELOW: *Shroud and gland compression nut.*

Score around armour.

BELOW LEFT: Remove armour.

Step 5
Cut away the outer sheath of the cable from where you have just scored it to the end that is to be terminated; a sharp knife should be used for this. Once the sheath has been removed, flex the strands of armour a couple of times where it has been scored and it will break off and leave a clean edge. (As with anything else, this may require a bit of practice.)

Step 6
About 25mm from the edge of the steel armour, score round the outer sheath using a knife; make sure that you cut through to the armour. Now cut along the section that has been cut through and remove it.

Step 7
Hold the outer sheath of the cable in one hand and then with the other hand move the stripped part of the cable round in a circle; this will spread the wire strands out slightly. Now slide the remaining part of the cable gland down over the cable, ensuring that all of the wire strands are over the tapered rough edge.

Step 4
Using the junior hacksaw, score around the cable following the line of the cable insulation; make sure that you cut only part-way through the steel armour. If you cut right through, there is a danger that you will also cut through the cable conductors.

Step 8
Screw the compression nut onto the large section of the gland, ensuring that all of the steel strands are captured between it and the gland. Use the gland nut pliers to tighten this section of the gland.

Outer sheath removed.

BELOW: *Spread out wire armour.*

Gland tightened using gland nut pliers or spanners.

Cable stripped back ready for termination.

Step 9

Using a knife, score around the inner section of the cable; this needs to be done with care to avoid cutting through the conductor insulation. Now bend the cable around where it has been scored and it should tear through the remaining depth. This section of insulation should now pull off. If it is difficult, use a knife to cut through the end and pull it off using a pair of pliers.

The cable is now ready for its final termination.

SINGLE CONDUCTORS IN CONDUIT OR TRUNKING

This type of cable is normally used in commercial or industrial installations as, unlike the other cables we have looked at, it needs to be provided with mechanical protection; usually this is plastic or steel conduit or trunking. These cables are manufactured in all standard cable sizes with the smallest being 1.5mm^2. It is usual for these cables to be stranded; this is to ensure that they are as flexible as possible for pulling into a conduit, which may contain bends.

Single PVC insulated cable.

DOUBLE-INSULATED SINGLE CONDUCTORS

These types of cables are usually for the connection of a consumer's unit to the supplier's meter and are referred to as tails.

HI TUFF

Hi Tuff cable looks very similar to SWA and in fact can be used as an alternative to SWA, as long as it is not going to be buried directly into the ground. The difference between the two cables is that Hi Tuff does not have a steel wire protective layer inside but it has an outer sheath that is made of very tough PVC. Because the cable does not have a steel sheath, one of the cores of the cable has to be used as a CPC.

This cable is cheaper than SWA and is much easier to terminate, as it simply requires stripping and terminating into a sealed plastic compression gland. No special tools are required; a knife and a pair of pliers are usually sufficient for this job.

Step 1
Measure and cut the cable to length and mark on the cable where the gland is to be fitted.

ABOVE: Meter tails.

BELOW LEFT: Hi Tuff.

BELOW RIGHT: Cable marked ready for stripping.

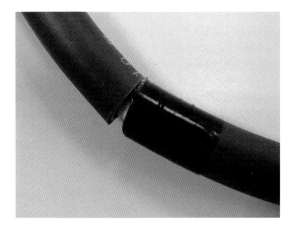

Outer sheath cut through.

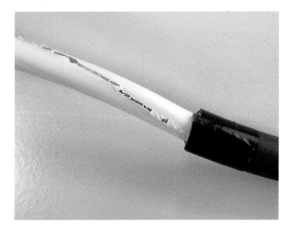

Outer sheath removed.

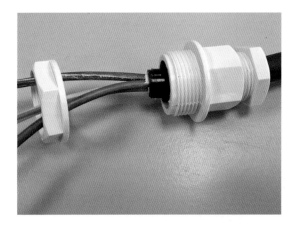

Inner sheath removed.

Score around the outer sheath with a knife, which will need to be sharp as the sheath is very hard. If the temperature is very low it may be better to warm the cable up first. Now flex the cable around the area that has been scored and the outer sheath should tear apart.

Step 2
Cut off the outer sheath. It may be possible to pull this off, if not, use pliers or, in some instances, it may have to be cut off very carefully.

Step 3
Once the outer sheath has been removed, the inner section of the cable will be exposed. At a distance of about 10mm from the outer sheath, score around the inner insulation. Care must be taken to ensure that the conductor insulation is not cut. Now flex the cable around the section that has been scored and the insulation should tear right through. Remove this section of insulation to expose the coloured conductor insulation.

The cable gland can now be fitted.

MINERAL INSULATED METAL CLAD CABLE (MICC)

This cable is also referred to as 'pyro', although this is a manufacturers' name for it, for the first company to supply this in the UK, which is called Pyrotenax.

The cable consists of solid copper conductors that are embedded in a powder known as magnesium oxide; the outer sheath around this cable is also copper. Due to the particular construction of this type of cable, it will not contribute to the spread of fire. It is also mechanically robust and resistant to impact. It can be flattened with a hammer and still operate perfectly well. It will also operate at very high temperatures. Often the cable is PVC-coated, as this will provide protection against corrosion. When the cable has a PVC coating, it can be purchased in various colours: orange, white, and red are the most common.

Orange would be used for general-purpose installations, white would be for emergency lighting or extra-low voltage circuits, and red would be used for fire alarm circuits.

Mineral insulated cable.

The main use for this cable is for fire protection. It is often used in buildings of great importance, or where important documents are kept, e.g. churches, museums and council buildings.

For installations such as petrol filling stations, oil refineries and other installations where there may be hazardous concentrations of flammable gas or high temperatures, MICC is the only choice of cable; although in these installations, the cables must be terminated using fire-rated glands.

The cable can be obtained with all of the same conductor sizes as other cables and have up to nineteen cores, possibly more if ordered specially. There are two ratings of cable, light duty and heavy duty, and the cables are identified using a numbering system.

Although this is a very good cable, it has some disadvantages. If bare copper cable is used, it is very prone to corrosion and consideration should be given to this before installing it. As it is copper, it can work-harden if bent too many times. The bending radius must not be tighter than six times the cable radius if it is to be bent more than once, or three times its diameter if bent only once.

The magnesium oxide is very hydroscopic and if the cable is left with unsealed ends it will absorb moisture; this will reduce the insulation resistance of the cable to levels that are unacceptable. Perhaps the biggest put-off to its use is that the termination of the cable is often seen as difficult and requires the use of special tools.

To terminate the cable correctly, the cable outer copper sheath must be removed. There are several ways in which this can be achieved.

Numbering Systems for Identifying Cable

Example 1: 2L1.5

1st character is the number of cores.
2nd character is the duty.
3rd character is the conductor CSA.
The example given would be a two-core, light duty with 1.5mm^2 conductors.

Example 2: 4H6
Four-core, heavy duty 6mm^2.

Step 1
The easiest method is to use an MI stripping tool to strip off as much of the copper sheath as required.

Step 2
Once stripped the gland shroud, the compression nut and olive and gland must be slipped onto the cable.

Stripping copper sheath.

Step 3
The pot must now be screwed onto the outer sheath of the cable. The conductors should be pulled firmly with a pair of pliers to ensure that the conductor is straight. Now place the seal over the conductors and slide it to within 25mm of the pot.

Now fill the pot with the sealing compound, (from one side only), being careful not to touch it with your fingers. This is because the conductors are so close together that any dirt or moisture on your fingers may result in a low insulation resistance being introduced to the cable.

TOP LEFT: *Gland and shroud on cable.*

MIDDLE LEFT: *Conductors pulled to straighten them.*

TOP RIGHT: *Seal placed on conductors.*

LEFT: *Sealing compound pushed into pot.*

Once you are sure that the pot is completely full, with all of the air expelled, push the seal down onto the top of the pot and use the compression tool to squeeze the seal tightly onto the pot.

Now cut the neoprene sleeving to the required length and slide over the conductors onto the seal.

Compression tool fixing securing seal to pot.

BELOW: Neoprene sleeving.

FP200 CABLE

This type of cable is generally used for fire alarm and emergency lighting circuits. The conductors can be solid or stranded and range from 1mm^2 up to 4mm^2. The live conductors are covered in a material called insudite, which is a fire-resistant insulating material; when it does burn it coats the conductor with an insulating ash. The CPC is bare just as you would find in flat twin and earth.

Around the outside of the insudite there is a layer of aluminium tape, which is metal side down touching the CPC. The mechanical protection around the outside of the cable is a casing of low smoke thermoplastic (LSF) material.

There are no special tools required to terminate FP200; where it enters an enclosure it should be terminated using a plastic compression gland.

Although this cable has a layer of aluminium tape around the cable cores, it should not be used for embedding directly into plaster, as the tape will not provide the required protection. In installations where this type of cable is to be buried, it must be RCD-protected or enclosed in an earthed metal containment system. However, most manufacturers do make a cable of this type, which is suitable for placing directly into plaster or stud partitions. BATT produce a cable known as Guardian Ali tube and FP 200 gold is also suitable.

This cable has a bare CPC enclosed with the other conductors, which are all encased in a thin aluminium tube. Special tools are not required to terminate this type of cable and, just for FP200, a compression gland should be used where the cable enters an enclosure.

ABOVE: *FP 200.*

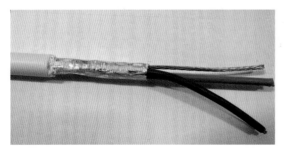

FP 200 gold suitable for embedding in plaster.

CHAPTER 6

Installation Methods

Cables can be installed using a variety of methods. Of course the installation method chosen must be suitable for the environment in which it is going to be used. Cost is also a factor that should be considered, particularly if you are a contractor trying to price for work competitively. Do remember that any cable that is buried into a wall and is unprotected by earthed metal must be protected by the installation of a residual current device; this must be installed at the supply end of the cable.

Most cables other than single-insulated cables, which must be mechanically protected by conduit or trunking, can be clipped directly to a surface with no mechanical protection other than that which is provided by the cable sheath. Any cable that is fixed to a surface does not need to be protected by an RCD, as it is unlikely that anybody will drive a nail though it by accident.

Where cables are to be buried out of sight in walls or under floors, they must be installed correctly.

Cables can be installed under floors, in ceiling spaces, lofts and in fact almost any building voids. The main consideration is that the cable is secured so as to ensure that it is never under any strain. Cables can be laid horizontally under a floor resting on a ceiling board, or in a loft fixed to the side of a joist, but they must not be permitted to hang vertically supporting their own weight, as over a period

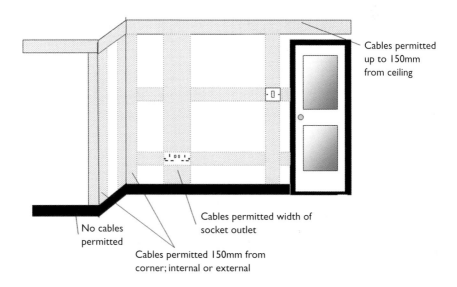

Cables permitted up to 150mm from ceiling

No cables permitted

Cables permitted width of socket outlet

Cables permitted 150mm from corner; internal or external

Permitted zones.

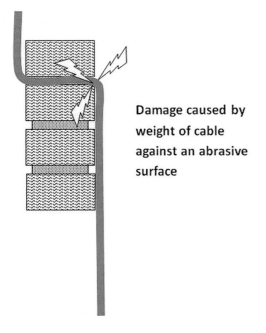

Damage caused by weight of cable against an abrasive surface

Cable supporting its own weight.

of time damage could occur. This is one reason why a cable must never be installed in a cavity of a building for anything other than very short distances; it is impossible to repair a cable that is hanging in a cavity. When using PVC cable, it is also very important to prevent the cable having contact with expanded polystyrene as this will make the cable very brittle over a short period of time.

Flat PVC cables can be installed in stud partitions but again, if they are vertical, they should be fixed suitably; they should also be RCD-protected. Where the cable is to be terminated into an accessory box, the box can be fixed into the stud partition by using a metal box fixed to a timber noggin or a box called a dry wall box can be used. This box has a lip around the front of the box to prevent it from falling right through the hole. It also has retractable fixing lugs, which push out behind the plasterboard; these lugs pull tight against the inside of the wall board when the accessory fixing screws are tightened.

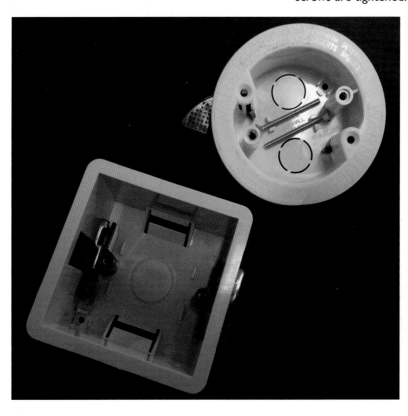

Round and square dry wall box.

PLASTIC AND STEEL CAPPING

Where it is required to plaster cables into a wall, there is no regulatory requirement for them to have any mechanical protection, other than that provided by the outer sheath of the cable. This is provided that the cables are protected by a residual current device (RCD). However, it is considered good practice to cover the cables with a mechanical protection that is rather stronger than the cable.

Capping is the cheapest and possibly the simplest method of protection, and when it is secured over a cable, it will protect it from the plasterer's trowel, which can, and occasionally does, cut through the outer sheath and inner insulation. The capping, if installed correctly, will allow the cable to be pulled out if required, when alterations are being carried out.

Capping can be obtained in galvanized steel or plastic and it is shaped into a channel of various widths.

The simplest way to install a cable into a wall using capping is to fix the accessory box first; this type of box is known as a knock-out box. This is

ABOVE RIGHT: Capping metal and plastic.

Knock-out boxes for setting into walls.

Knock-out box set in wall with grommet fitted.

over the cable or cables, making sure that it reaches right down to the top of the box. Now the capping can be secured back to the wall using small corrosion-resistant pins; small plasterboard nails are ideal for this job.

The wall can now be plastered and the cable will remain safe. An RCD must also be installed when this method is used.

Capping is more suited for use on walls before they are plastered, rather than on a wall that has had the plaster cut away.

PLASTIC OVAL CONDUIT

The installation of cables using this method is very popular as the conduit completely encases the cable or cables, while allowing them to be plastered into a wall with the minimum of chasing out. This method also allows the cables to be drawn out of the conduit if alterations are required at a later date. Where cables are installed using this method, they must be protected by the use of a residual current device (RCD).

Oval conduit can be obtained in a variety of sizes, and the size you use will depend on the size and number of cables that you need to install. This type of conduit will protrude from the wall a little more than capping, and occasionally a very shallow channel may need to be cut into the wall to allow the conduit to be recessed slightly, to ensure that it can be covered by the plaster.

because there are cable entry holes on all sides and the back; the hole which you want to use for your cable entry simply has to be knocked out.

The box can be fixed using plugs and screws or it can be set into the wall using plaster or cement. If you use plaster or cement, you will have to wait until it is set before putting the cables in. This is a good method of fixing boxes for larger jobs because you can fix the box and run the cabling round to the points the day before fixing the cables to the wall. Whichever method you use, make sure that the box will end up flush with the plaster, as if it is set too deep the accessory screws will not be long enough. Usually leaving the box protruding slightly more than the capping will generally be sufficient.

Ensure that the route that the cable is going to take into the box is free from rough edges. It is advisable to give the wall a good scrape with a floor bolster to make absolutely sure it is free of any lumps of cement. Next, lay the cable down the wall through the hole in the top of the box. The hole must have an open grommet placed into it, to protect the cables from the sharp edges of the hole.

The cable must be run either horizontally or vertically from the box. The capping is then placed

Once again, it is easier if the box is fixed first using one of the methods described previously, including the fitting of a grommet. Ensure that the area in which the cable will be running is free from protruding mortar. Cut the conduit to length, allowing enough for it to touch the box and for 30mm to 50mm to be above the ceiling. Thread the cables into the conduit and then through the grommet into the box. Now hold the conduit back to the wall to check that it is not going to stick out above the plaster.

Providing the conduit is set back enough, it can now be fixed. The easiest method is to use galvanized plasterboard nails. Fix the conduit each side at suitable positions, allowing just the head of the nail to pinch the side of the conduit. At the same time, ensure that the nail heads are set back far enough to miss the plaster. Do not be tempted to use nails that could rust, as this will show through the paint or wallpaper.

MINI-TRUNKING

There are various reasons why cables cannot be hidden, not least it may be that the customer does not want their decoration damaged. In these cases, a good installation method is to use plastic mini-trunking. This trunking comes in many sizes and will accommodate PVC flat twin cable comfortably. It can be fixed back to surfaces using screws or even small tacks, if required. Self-adhesive trunking is also available; this has a sticky back and will fix very well to most clean surfaces. Various fittings can be used with this trunking to make it as neat as possible.

This type of trunking can also be used for singles cable, if required. Any circuits that are installed using this method would not require the installation of an RCD for additional protection, unless of course the circuit required this type of protection for another reason.

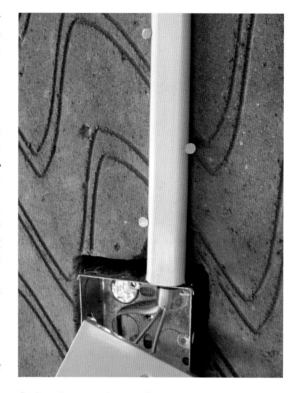

Oval conduit secured to a wall.

Mini-trunking.

Mini-trunking fittings.

ROUND PLASTIC CONDUIT

Round plastic conduit is a very versatile type of containment system. Where it is used in plastered walls, the wall must be chased out first to a depth that is suitable to prevent the conduit showing above the plaster. Using this method of installation requires a little more work but the end result is that the cables can be pulled out for alterations or rewires very easily.

The tools required to chase out a wall are:

• Club hammer.
• Cold chisel.
• Floor bolster.
• Tape measure.
• Spirit-level.
• Goggles.
• Gloves, if you are not very skilled with the hammer.

Before you start, check on the other side of the wall to see if there are any ornaments or pictures, which may fall off any shelves or edges, as when you start chasing you will create a bit of vibration.

Mark the position of the accessory box and then draw a line where the chase is required; this will require the use of a spirit-level, as the chase needs to be as straight as possible. The easiest way to cut a neat chase is to hold the cold chisel with the cutting edge horizontal against the wall at the bottom of the line and cut about 5mm of the wall out at a time, working your way up. Like anything else, you may find an easier way. Some electricians prefer to use an attachment fitted to a percussion drill, although this method does not suit me. Any method is fine, as long as the end result is satisfactory.

Boxes can be cut into the wall using much the same method, or tools are available that attach to a percussion drill, which cut a neat hole for knock-out boxes with the minimum of effort.

Once the chasing has been completed, the cables can be threaded through the conduit, and then through the knock-out of the box, which of course must have a grommet fitted. The box and the conduit can now be put into position and fixed back. Again, plasterboard nails used to pinch the conduit is the easiest method and the box can be secured

ABOVE: Box set into wall with conduit fixed.
LEFT: Wall being chased out.

as previously explained. Remember to allow the box to protrude to the depth of the plaster.

This type of conduit can also be used on the surface and is particularly useful for many types of installations, including small workshops and corrosive environments.

PVC conduit is available as light or heavy duty, and the standard colours are white or black. Black conduit is the most suited for use outdoors, as it is unaffected by the sun's UV rays.

Where round plastic conduit is used for complete installations, it is easier and cheaper to use singles cable. Various types of conduit fittings can be used for the installation and it is important that the conduit system is completed before any wiring is drawn into it.

This type of conduit can also be bent using a tool called a bending spring.

Before attempting to bend the conduit, the section to be bent must first be warmed up. The simplest way is to use friction and rub it hard with a gloved hand or a piece of rag.

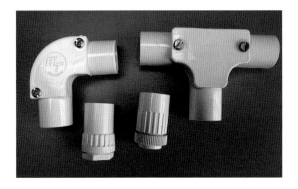

ABOVE: Plastic conduit fittings.

RIGHT: Bending spring inserted into conduit.

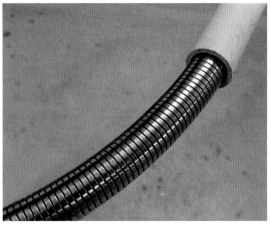

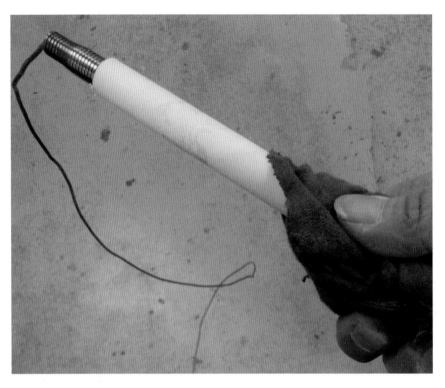

Conduit being warmed using friction.

Once the conduit is warm, insert the spring to the desired depth and bend the conduit over your knee. This may need to be done in sections, as the bending radius must be no greater than 2.5 times the diameter of the conduit. Always over-bend the conduit, as you will find that it tends to straighten out a bit when you let it go.

When installing this type of system, it is a good idea to fit the accessory boxes into position first, where possible. Once the boxes are fitted, a spirit-level can be used to mark out where the saddles are to be fixed.

The conduit can now be installed in sections between using conduit fittings, as required. Inspection elbows, bends or boxes should be used to enable the cables to be drawn into the conduit system when it is complete. To ensure that all parts of the system are secure, the fittings should be attached to the conduit using a special solvent adhesive. Where the installation requires a long run of

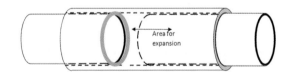

Expansion coupler.

Distances between fixings.

Nominal size of conduit	Maximum distance between supports	
Diameter (mm)	Horizontal (m)	Vertical (m)
Not exceeding 16	0.75	1.0
Exceeding 16 but not exceeding 25	1.5	1.75
Exceeding 25 but not exceeding 40	1.75	2.0
Exceeding 40	2.0	2.0

Drawing in tape.

conduit, it is important to remember that plastic conduit expands and contracts in length, depending on the temperature; an allowance should be made to accommodate this movement and an expansion coupler should be fitted.

The coupler should be glued to one end of the conduit and left free on the other end. Be carful that the conduit is not pushed completely into the coupler, particularly on a cold day, as room must be left to allow it to expand when the temperature changes.

Once the conduit has been installed, the cables can be installed into the conduit. A drawing in tape

should be used for longer sections or for multiple circuits.

Wherever possible use stranded cables, as these are very much more flexible than solid stranded cables. It is also a good idea to pull all of the cables, which are to be installed into a particular section of the system, into the conduit at the same time.

When cables are pulled into conduits that already have cables in, there is a risk that the cables already installed could be damaged due to the new cables rubbing against them and causing friction, which will burn through the insulation. In installations where cables already exist, it is important that the conduit is large enough to contain the additional circuits; if it is, the cables must be drawn in slowly. Very often the use of French chalk or even talcum powder will make the installation a little easier.

FIXINGS

If we are going to install electrical equipment, it is important to be aware of the different types of fixings that are available and how they should be used correctly.

Wood Screws

These come in various sizes with different-shaped heads. Most wood screws purchased now will be in metric measurements, although on occasion it is useful to know how they compare.

The screw heads are usually slotted or cross-head. Cross-head are often referred to as Phillips or posidrive. The correct type of screwdriver must

Comparison of metric and imperial wood screws.

Diameter		Common Lengths		Clearance Hole		Pilot Hole	
Gauge	Metric	Imperial (in)	Metric (mm)	Imperial (in)	Metric (mm)	Imperial (in)	Metric (mm)
2	2.0	¼–½	6.5–13	³/₃₂	2.5	¹/₁₆	1.6
3	2.5	³/₈–1	10–25	⁷/₆₄	3.0	¹/₁₆	1.6
4	3.0	¼–1½	6.5–38	⅛	3.5	⁵/₆₄	2.0
6	3.5	³/₈–2½	10–65	⁵/₃₂	4.0	⁵/₆₄	2.0
8	4.0	³/₈–3¼	10–90	³/₁₆	5.0	³/₃₂	2.5
10	5.0	½–4	13–100	⁷/₃₂	5.75	⅛	3.5
12	5.5	¾–5	19–125	¼	6.5	⅛	3.5
14	6.5	1¼–6	32–150	¼	6.5	⁵/₃₂	4.0

Posidrive or Phillips screw.

Counter-sunk screw.

Round head screw.

always be used, as this will prevent the head of the screw being damaged, as well as making the turning of the screw easier – particularly if it is a bit on the tight side.

The shape of the head of the screw will depend on what the screw is being used for. There are many different types of screw head and the three most common, and the types that we are most likely to use, are:

- Counter-sunk. These have a flat head, which allows them to be fixed with the head flush to the surface of the material being fixed.
- Round head. These screw down on to a flat surface with the head remaining on show.
- Raised head. This type of screw is counter-sunk and has a raised head. This is the type of head that is used on socket and switch screws.

These screws are manufactured using many types of metals. The type used is dependent on what it is being used for.

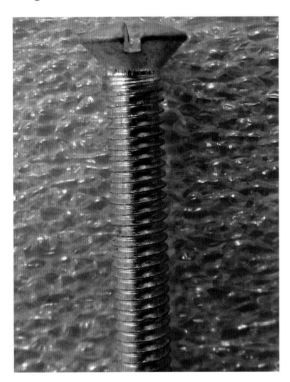

Raised head screw.

For general use, a steel screw would be used. If the screw was for an outdoor installation, a brass or stainless-steel screw could be used. Screws are also produced with many kinds of decorative finishes, such as chrome, polished brass and bronze.

Fixing to Wood

Where this type of screw is used to fix equipment to a wooden surface, it is advisable to drill a pilot hole first, particularly if the wood is of the hard wood variety. The table provides guidelines as to which size pilot hole is suitable for a particular size of screw.

Fixing to Solid Walls

When using wood screws to fix to a brick or solid surface, a hole should be drilled into the surface using a masonry drill to make a hole into which a plastic fixing plug is pushed. There are many types, sizes and colours of plastic plugs available, but whichever type you use, it is essential that the correct size of plastic plug is used to suit the screw and the correct size of drill is used to suit the plug.

If the wall is a hard material, then it will be necessary to use a percussion or hammer drill. With the correct type of masonry bit it is no problem to drill into any type of construction material including concrete.

The most common types of plastic plugs are supplied in four colours, which can be used to identify the correct type of plug to suit the size of screw being used.

- Yellow plugs will fit into a 5mm hole and would be suitable for screw sizes 4–8.
- Red plugs will fit into a 6mm hole and are suitable for screw sizes 6–10.
- Brown plugs will fit into a 7mm hole and are for screw sizes 10–14.
- Blue plugs will fit into a 10mm hole and are suitable for screw sizes 14–18.

Always ensure that the hole is deep enough to allow the screw to be tightened fully and, when inserting the plug, make sure the top of the plug is pushed into the hole past the surface of the wall to help prevent the plaster breaking away from the surface of the wall.

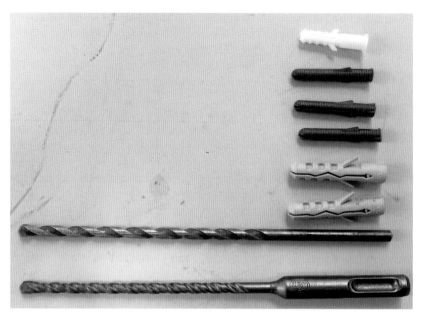

Masonry drill and plastic wall plugs.

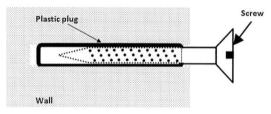

Plug and screw inserted into wall.

Fixing Through Glazed Tiles

When a fixing has to be made through a glazed tile, care must be taken. Although it is not a difficult job if carried out properly using the right tools, there is always the possibility of breaking the tile if you get it wrong.

It is possible to use a masonry bit to drill through the tile; a new drill is the best bet as it will be sharp. If you try to drill a tile with an old masonry drill you will probably end up shattering the tile.

Drill bits that are made especially for drilling through glazed tiles can also be used.

Method
Mark the position of the hole using a marker pen (some tiles are difficult to mark with a pencil). To prevent the bit slipping around at the start, it is a good idea to place a piece of tape over the tile where the hole is to be drilled.

Gently place the tip of the bit onto the mark, push on the drill firmly and allow it to rotate slowly.

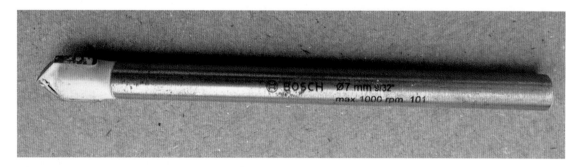

Drill bit for glazed tiles.

If using a power drill, do not use the hammer function. Providing the drill is sharp, it will begin to cut through the glaze on the tile. Do not push too hard, as the point at which you are drilling the tile may not have any adhesive behind it. Once the bit has cut through the glaze, speed the drill up a bit but do not use the hammer function unless you are certain that the tile is supported by adhesive. A sharp bit will easily cut through the tile.

Once through the tile and the bit is against the wall, the hammer function can be used. It is a good idea to pull the bit out of the hole occasionally to clear the material that has been drilled out of the hole. Doing this will extend the life of the bit quite considerably.

When you are satisfied that the hole is deep enough, the plastic plug can be pushed into it. The plastic plug must be pushed right through the tile; this is because when the screw is wound into the plug, it will expand, and if the end of the plug is in the tile, the tile will split. Do not be afraid to use a light tap with a hammer to drive the plug through the tile. A screw can be used as a punch for the last few millimetres of the process.

Anchor Bolts

Where it is required to fix a heavy piece of equipment to the floor or a wall, anchor bolts can be used. This type of bolt fits into a pre-drilled hole and when tightened, the sides of the bolt expands against the side of the hole.

Rawl bolt or anchor bolt.

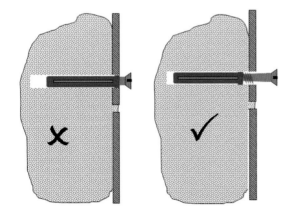

Plug pushed into wall past tile.

There are various types of anchor bolts manufactured to suit many types of applications. As with any other fixing that requires a hole to be drilled, it is very important that the hole is the correct size.

Fixing to Plasterboard and Hollow Walls

There are many different types of fixings available for fixing to surfaces that have not got a solid backing to fix into. Before fixing to any hollow surface, the first consideration must be to ensure that it is strong enough to support whatever it is that is to be fixed to it.

Noggin for supporting luminaire.

The electrical wiring regulations suggest that any fixing for light fittings must be able to support a minimum mass of 5kg; in some instances this may require the installation of a noggin.

BELOW: Butterfly toggle bolt.

Toggle Bolt

Toggle bolts are probably the most used plaster-board fixing and there are two types. Both are difficult to remove once they have been installed.

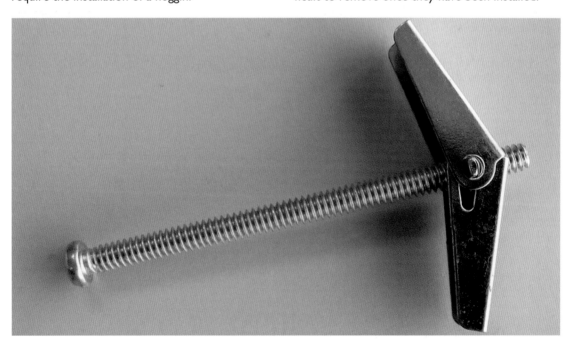

Gravity toggle bolt.

Butterfly or spring toggle bolts are pushed through a pre-drilled hole in the board and when the toggles are right through, they spring out. As the screw is tightened, they pull against the inner surface of the board and hold whatever it is being fixed secure.

Gravity toggle bolts are pushed through the pre-drilled holes. This type of bolt will only have one loose toggle, which relies on its own weight to open it once it is through the hole. The disadvantage of using toggle bolts is that once the screw is removed the toggle drops to the bottom of the wall.

Plasterboard anchors are a very good type of permanent fixing for plasterboard or hollow partitions. They are inserted into a pre-drilled hole in the board and then tightened. As they are tightened, the metal sleeve or rubber is squashed, which makes it expand onto the back of the board. Once it is fixed, it remains in place, even when the screw is removed.

Self-drilling plasterboard fixings can be used for most applications and are probably the easiest and quickest to use; they simply have to be screwed into the board using a cross-head screwdriver. Once inserted into the board, they can be used as a screw fixing; they can also be removed by being unscrewed if they are no longer required.

Plasterboard anchor.

ACCESSORY BOXES

Unless the electrical equipment that you are installing is self-contained, it will need to be fitted to a box of some sort. On occasions it will be useful to have a box to which self-contained equipment can be fixed to.

There are many different types of box and, of course, it makes life easier if we know what is available and also the correct name for it. A selection of the most common are included here, with an explanation of what they can be used for. The electrical wiring regulations state that wherever electrical connections are made, they must be contained within an enclosure; these boxes can form that enclosure.

Single Gang Surface Plastic Box

These boxes come in different depths and are used to fit switches and single socket outlets onto a surface, as well as numerous other items, such as fused connection units and flex outlets. Deeper boxes can be used for 45a cord switches.

ABOVE LEFT: Self-drilling plasterboard fixing.

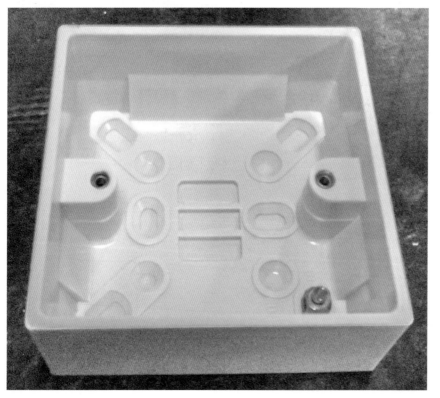

Single gang surface box.

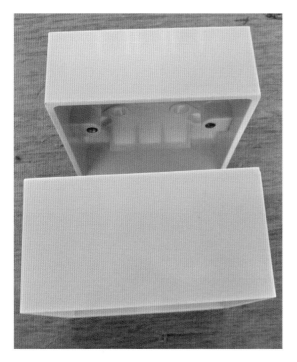

Deep single gang plastic box.

Double Surface Plastic Box

These boxes come in various depths and are most commonly used for twin-socket outlets, or providing the deeper type is selected, it could be used to fix a surface cooker switch or shower switch.

Two Gang Surface Plastic Box

This type of box is used where two single accessories are required next to each other, possibly a one gang single socket outlet, which requires a fuse connection unit next to it.

Surface Plastic Architrave Box

This box would be used where there is not enough space to install a traditional switch; the switch used is called an architrave switch.

Plastic Back Plates For Surface Mounted Light Fittings

It is not acceptable to connect a light fitting using connectors and then screwing the light back, leaving the connectors against a combustible

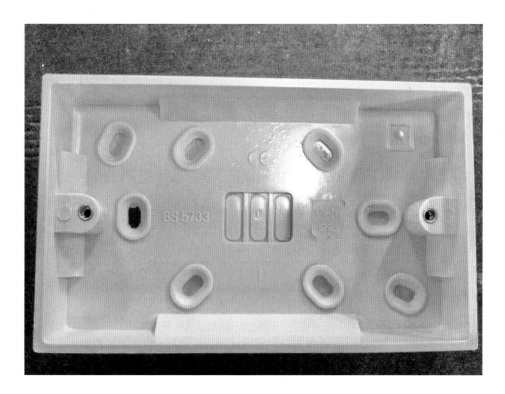

Double plastic surface box.

Deep double plastic surface box.

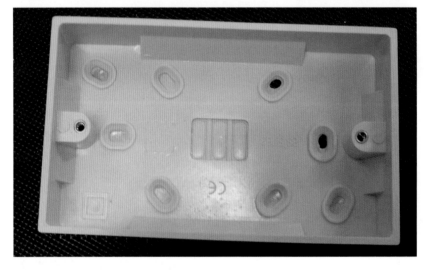

Two gang plastic surface box.

surface such as a ceiling. All connections must be contained in a non-combustible enclosure, and for this reason a thin plastic back plate is made, which fits onto the surface above the light fitting forming an enclosure.

Flush Plasterboard Box

These boxes come in the same sizes as the surface mounted boxes, and are intended to fit into the plasterboard on a stud wall. A hole has to be cut into the wall to suit the size of the box being used. They have a lip around the front edge to prevent them from falling through the hole

and, once the box has been pushed into the wall, the screw fixing lugs push out onto the inside of the wall. When the accessory screws are tightened, the box pulls tight and everything is held secure.

Single Gang Metal Knock-Out Boxes

These are buried into a wall or floor and can be used to fix any single accessory to a wall. When using metal boxes it is always very important to fit an open grommet to prevent the cables being damaged by sharp edges.

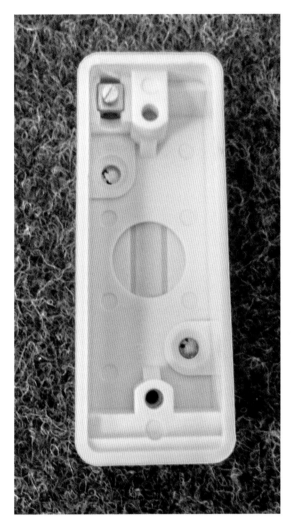

ABOVE: Surface plastic architrave box.

ABOVE RIGHT: Plastic back plate for light fittings.

MIDDLE RIGHT: Plasterboard boxes.

BOTTOM RIGHT: Single knock-out box.

Double Metal Knock-Out Boxes

These are usually used for double-socket outlets but they can also be used for multiple switches contained on one switch plate or switch grid.

Metal Architrave Box

These boxes were originally produced to allow a switch to be installed into an architrave. These days they are used where space is tight or even simply for decorative purposes.

Round Plastic Conduit Boxes

These boxes are used to terminate or change the direction of plastic conduit. The screw holes are the same distance apart as the fixings for ceiling roses, batten holders, pull cords and various other items of equipment. They form a perfect enclosure for electrical connections and they can be installed on the surface or flushed into walls, floors or ceilings.

TOP: *Double knock-out box.*

ABOVE: *Metal architrave box.*

Round Metal Conduit Boxes

These boxes can be used for the same equipment as the plastic round boxes and are normally used with threaded conduit.

Plastic conduit boxes.

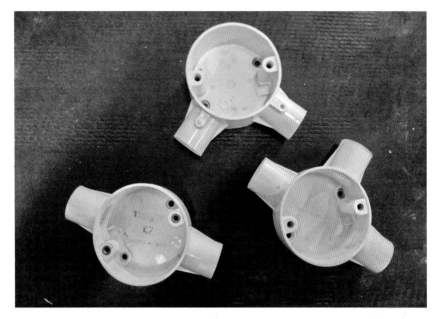

Metal conduit boxes.

CHAPTER 7

Planning an Electrical Job

Before embarking on any kind of electrical work it is important that the correct preparation is carried out; this is in many ways one of the most important parts of the job.

Regardless of whether it is a large or small job the basic preparation is the same.

It is important to ascertain that the installation that we are going to work on, or connect to, is safe and suitable for any addition; never add to an installation that is unsafe. We also need information about the supply system, as on completion of any work, a certificate will need to be produced.

It is always worthwhile planning thoroughly and considering all of the different options that may be available. These may revolve around cost, time or even the upheaval and damage to decorated areas.

Most electricians have a mental checklist, which they perform from the moment they step onto a job.

The first consideration is for personal safety and safety of others:

- Are the areas in which we are going to work safe?
- Will any personal protective equipment be required?
- Is access equipment required?
- Are there any heavy items to be moved?
- Will the building/room be occupied while work is being carried out?
- Will it be possible to isolate the parts of the installation being worked on?

Once you have ascertained that the work can be carried out safely, you can start planning other aspects of the job. It is time well spent just thinking about what you are going to do. For example:

- How long do you think the job will take? Always allow enough time.
- Will the work damage any of the decoration?
- How many dust sheets will be required?
- For how long will you need to isolate parts or all of the system?
- If you need to isolate the system, will there be adequate lighting or power? Freezers can normally be turned off for a few hours but they cannot be left indefinitely and it may be necessary to provide a temporary supply.
- Have you the correct tools available to carry out the work correctly?

Planning the sequence in which you are going to carry out the work is vital; for example, if the work involves cutting out chases in the wall, try and do them at the same time. This will avoid making two or three messes.

If the work involves taking up floorboards, try and ensure that they are not left up for very long, especially if the building is occupied. The last thing you want is for someone to put their foot down the hole – it may harm them and they will certainly damage the ceiling below.

Cats love hiding under floors and more than once I have completed a job and then heard the cat trying to find a way out; this can prove very embarrassing for you and have even worse consequences for the cat.

A list of materials will need to be made and all of the items purchased before commencing the job, unless of course you have planned your job around it and it is something that you can fix later.

CABLE ROUTE

Always try and plan the cable route before you start, as this will help ensure that you have the correct materials and tools to hand.

When installing a cable there are three very important things to consider with regard to the route that the cable will take:

- It is best to keep the cable runs as short as possible.
- The cable must be protected from damage.
- The cable's current rating will be severely reduced if it gets hot; avoiding heat and thermal insulation is very important.

Of course it is always better to conceal the cable; this may involve chasing it into a wall and plastering over the cable. This may not be possible at the time the work is being carried out, as you may not want to damage the decoration. Always remember that the cable can be run on the surface and concealed at a later date.

When cables are to be installed on the surface, always keep them out of harm's way, particularly if the cable is to be unprotected. Cables that are clipped over a skirting are very vulnerable, as they are likely to be damaged by a vacuum cleaner or children's toys.

Cables buried in walls or concealed in areas where they cannot be seen must be dealt with very carefully. This is because if they cannot be seen, someone putting up a picture or drilling a hole for a fixing of some kind may not know that the cable is there. BS 7671 wiring regulations give us various options for when we are concealing cables.

Cables in Walls and Partitions

1. The cable can be buried to a depth of at least 50mm. The problem with this is that building regulations forbid us from cutting into a wall deeper than one-sixth of the wall thickness, where the chase is horizontal.

Where the chase is vertical, the chase is only permitted to be one-third of the wall thickness. Or

2. The cable must have earthed armouring or an earthed metal sheath. Steel-wired armoured cable, mineral insulated or FP 200 gold would be suitable. Or
3. It must be encased in earthed steel conduit or trunking. Or
4. Be provided with a form of protection, which will prevent penetration of nails, masonry drills and screws (this is very difficult to achieve). Or
5. Protect the cables by using a 30mA RCD.

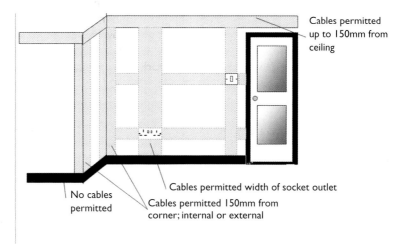

Cables permitted up to 150mm from ceiling

Cables permitted width of socket outlet

Cables permitted 150mm from corner; internal or external

No cables permitted

Cable zones.

It is also recommended that the cables are installed in zones vertically above or below outlets and switches, or horizontally either side of them. If it is necessary to run cables across walls or from the bottom to the top of the wall, they must be installed within 150mm of the ceiling. All cables that are not installed as described in 1–4 must be protected by an RCD.

Many buildings have partitions that use metal stud/framing. Cables installed in these partitions must be installed as recommended in 2, 3 or 4, or be RCD-protected.

To keep it simple, it is better to protect all circuits using an RCD, unless there is a very good reason not to.

Cables Installed in Floors or Ceilings

Wherever we install cables we must always consider whether or not they might be damaged. This damage could occur from the ceiling, the floor or any fixings that may be used. Just because we can't see them, it does not mean that they are safe.

Cables can be threaded through joists or laid on top of them in notches, providing that they comply with the following rules:

1. Be at least 50mm from the top or the bottom (for a notch this would be impossible to achieve in most instances). Or
2. Be enclosed in earthed conduit or trunking. Or
3. The cable must have an earthed metal sheath. Or
4. Be protected from penetration by nails or screws.

Clearly item 4 is very difficult to achieve and the use of notches should be avoided, if possible. There

are going to be occasions where the use of a notch is unavoidable, particularly where a cable is to be run through a joist that has already been cut.

Never be tempted to drill a hole for a cable through a roof rafter!!

Approved document A provides practical guidance on the drilling and notching of joists.

Where a joist has already been drilled or notched, it would be pretty pointless to drill it again, where the hole is in a dangerous area, i.e. near the top or bottom. It is better to use the existing hole and take precautions against the penetration of a screw or a nail.

If a new hole is required, then we must always consider whether the joist will be weakened. Where there is a notch, we would not be permitted to drill a hole in the same area because we might weaken it. If we cannot change the cable route, then protection against penetration by nails or screws must be provided. This is very difficult to achieve and this method of installation is always best to avoid. Where it cannot be avoided, always mark the position of the cables on the floor above the cable.

Never be tempted to run cables alongside heating or water pipes. Any heat produced by the water in the pipes will not only have a major effect on the current-carrying capabilities of the cable, it will also damage the insulation.

Thermal Insulation

Where a cable is touching or surrounded by thermal insulation, the current-carrying capacity of the cable will be reduced. This is because the heat created by the current passing through the conductor

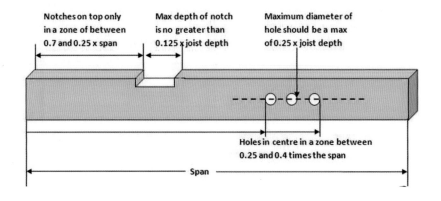

Drilling or notching joists.

will be unable to dissipate through the insulation. For this reason, contact with thermal insulation should be avoided where possible. Of course, in some cases, contact with thermal insulation will be unavoidable and the current-carrying capacity will need to be calculated taking this into account. Information on cable calculation is provided in Chapter 11.

Multiple Circuits

Where the cable that is being installed is to be grouped in an enclosure containing other circuits, or bunched with other circuits, an allowance must also be made to take into account the temperature at which the other cables are operating. Where possible we should try and keep cables away from anything that may increase their temperature. Information on grouping is provided in Chapter 11.

Other Services

Wherever cables are installed, they must be protected from any harmful mutual effects. To ensure this does not happen, we must never fix cables to other services, such as gas or water pipes. On occasions, when it is impossible to avoid other services, the cable should be fixed far enough away to prevent any damage, should work need to be carried out on the services. In some cases, additional mechanical protection may be required.

Electrical equipment, such as consumer's units, must be kept at least 150mm away from gas services; electricity cables must be kept at least 25mm away from gas services.

Segregation of Voltages

Where voltages of different bands are present, i.e. Band I and Band II, they must not be contained in the same enclosure (trunking/conduit) unless:

- The conductors of different bands are installed into separate compartments. Or

- The conductors are insulated to the highest voltage present.
- If a multicore cable is used for different bands, each core must be insulated to the highest voltage present. Or
- If they are fixed to a cable tray, they must be separated by a partition.

Telephone Cables

Low-voltage electrical cables must always be kept a minimum distance of 50mm away from telephone cables, unless they are enclosed within a separate conduit or trunking. If the conduit or trunking is metallic, then it must be correctly earthed. Steel-wired armour and mineral insulated cables may also be used where segregation is required.

LIFTING FLOORING

Once we have carefully considered which route our cable is going to take, we may find that we will need to lift some flooring to gain access to the planned route.

There are generally two different types of flooring that we will come across: tongue and groove (T & G) flooring and chipboard flooring.

Tongue and Groove Flooring

T & G is a flat plank of wood with a groove cut into one side and a tongue on the other; the tongue of one board fits into the groove of the board next to it.

Once the boards are nailed down to the floor joists, which will be at right angles to the floorboard, this system provides a very good floor surface.

Lifting a section of board is a reasonably simple job, although care must be taken to ensure that you do not cut through any pipes or cables that may be below the floor. Obviously, before you start, a simple visual check will give an indication of whether there is likely to be anything, e.g. radiators or water pipes, nearby. A simple metal detector can also be used as a guide.

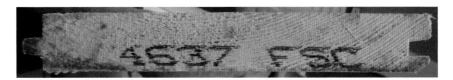

Tongue and groove flooring.

It is always easier to lift a board starting from a joint, if possible; if not, you will have to cut across the board at some point.

Step 1

Cut through the tongue on each side of the board. I prefer to use a floor bolster for this where possible. Hold the bolster along the tongue and knock it through using a hammer. The bolster will only need to go through the board about 25mm. Repeat this process along both sides of the board up to 150mm past the section that you want to lift.

If the boards are particularly tight together, you can also use a small circular saw. If you do, set the blade a little less than the thickness of the board; this will ensure that you don't cut through anything underneath. If you are using a bolster, you will feel or hear if you touch anything; this will not be the case if you use a circular saw. Never be tempted to use a jigsaw unless you are absolutely certain that nothing is underneath.

Step 2

At the end that has been cut, push the bolster through the floor and gently prise the board up. Repeat this process on the other side of the board and work your way along to the end. You will now

be able to look under the board and see what is there.

Step 3

Once you are sure that this is the board that will be the most useful to remove, place your bolster under the board across the gap, as far down the board as possible.

You can now saw through the board and remove it. Never leave the board lying around with nails in it – always remove them from the board and the joists before you do anything else.

When replacing the board, use screw fixings, if possible. Pre-drilling the board will prevent it from splitting.

Chipboard Flooring

Lifting chipboard flooring is a little more difficult than lifting T & G flooring because there are fewer joints in it. Also, once it is cut, the floor becomes quite weak and replacing it properly is very important. This type of flooring is usually 1200mm long and 60mm wide with a tapered groove on two sides and a tapered tongue on the other.

To remove a section, the same safety precautions must be carried out as for T & G. With this type of flooring, it is often slightly more difficult to see which way the floor joists run. Usually the joists run across the narrow part of the board but it is always a good idea to look for the board fixings – this will help you decide.

Step 1

For this job, a circular saw is the best tool. Set the blade carefully to the thickness of the board and mark the floor where you want to cut it. Once again, if you are not sure what is underneath the board, do not use a jigsaw, as there is always a possibility that you may damage a cable or a pipe.

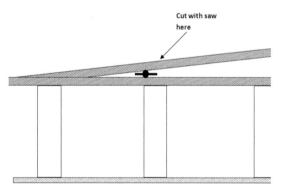

Cut with saw here

ABOVE LEFT: Lifting and cutting T & G flooring.

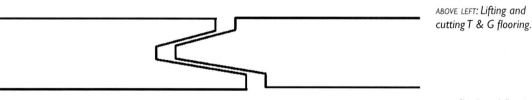

LEFT: Chipboard flooring.

Step 2
Carefully cut around the section of board that you need to remove. Where possible, cut along a joist, as this will help give some support when the section is replaced.

Step 3
Once the section of board has been cut around, it is a simple job just to lift it out. The section of board that is removed is commonly referred to as a trap.

Once the work has been completed, the trap will have to be replaced. If this is not done correctly, then it will be very weak and may break when it has any weight placed on it.

Where the edge of the trap fits back onto a floor joist, it will be secure; the problem arises when the board spans two or more joists – unsupported chipboard is not very strong and will break very easily.

The best way to ensure that the replaced trap is strong enough is to support it with timber fixed across the hole. This timber can be fixed by screws through the flooring that has not been removed. Always ensure that the supporting timber extends under the flooring far enough to allow it to be secured by at least three screws. If not, the screws will pull through the chipboard when any heavy load is placed on the trap.

DRILLING JOISTS

As previously mentioned, when drilling through joists, care must be taken to ensure that the joist is not weakened. Where you are adding to an existing installation, you may well find that a hole or a notch is already available for you to make use of; in these situations it is fine to use it.

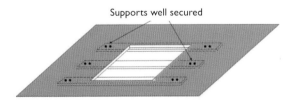

Supports well secured

Support for replacing of chipboard floor.

Selection of wood drill bits.

When it is necessary for you to drill a hole or a series of holes for your cable, the easiest method is to use an electric drill and a wood bit. There are various types of wood bits available and, of course, if they drill through wood, then the use of any of them would be fine.

Always ensure that the electric drill is powerful enough to do the job and that the wood bit is sharp. When drilling through a joist it is very unlikely that you will be able to drill a horizontal hole – the gap between the joists will not be enough to fit the drill into and it will have to be held at an angle.

Always start at least 50mm from the top of the joist and always check that there is nothing fixed to the other side of the joist that may be damaged when the drill bit passes through the joist. It is also very important to hold onto the electric drill very firmly and be ready when the drill bit passes through the back of the joist – it will probably 'grab' and either pull through very quickly or seize up; the electric drill will snatch out of your hands if you are unprepared.

Notching

Always avoid notching joists wherever possible and remember, if notching is unavoidable, then care must be taken to ensure that a screw or a nail cannot penetrate the cable at a later date. Always mark on the top of the board to show that there is a cable underneath.

Where notching is required, always make sure that the notch is cut in the centre of the section of the joist that is exposed. This will allow the board to be fixed back into position without the risk of damage to the cable.

To make a notch in a joist, cut through the joist with a wood saw to the required depth and width for the cable, and use a wood chisel to remove the section required.

Cables under Floors

Where cables are run under floors and do not have to pass through joists, they can be laid on ceilings or sub-floors. This is usually a very good route for cables, as they are out of harm's way. Where cables are placed under floors, it is not a requirement that the cables are fixed; this is because no strain will be placed on the cables, as they will be supported by the ceiling below or the sub-floor. When the cables are laid on a sub-floor, consideration must be given to protection from damage that may be caused by fauna (mice, rats, etc.). However, unless the cables can be clipped at the correct spacing, do not be tempted to hang the cable between clips at long distances apart just to keep the cable off the ground. This could strain the cable over a period of time.

The easiest method for threading cables under floors or in any kind of building voids is to use a special tool, called a fishing tool.

These tools are usually all insulated and can be screwed together for additional lengths, if required.

As with any other special tool, unless you are going to use it often, it can become expensive and for that reason sometimes it is a good idea to im-provise. On many occasions I have used a length of small plastic oval conduit or even a length of fence wire.

Cables in Roof Spaces and Lofts

Roof spaces and lofts are a good place to run ca-bles, as long as you give consideration to where in the roof the cables will be safe from any mechanical damage.

Points to consider:

- Never drill through roof rafters, as this will not only weaken the roof but also contravenes build-ing regulations. It is perfectly acceptable to fix cables to rafters.
- Never drill through or notch ceiling joists unless they are much larger than the standard 100mm deep.
- Never drill through any part of a roofing truss.
- Always try and keep the cables away from ther-mal insulation. Remember, any cable surrounded by thermal insulation for a length greater than 500mm will have its current-carrying capacity halved. If the cable is laid on top of the insulation, it will not be affected enough to give cause for concern, although, if it is laid onto a plasterboard ceiling with more than 100mm of thermal insula-tion placed on top of it, the cable will only be able to carry 65 per cent of its maximum capac-ity.
- Give some thought to where people may walk if they are in the loft/roof space.
- Always try and place the cable as close to the eaves of the roof as possible; this is because this area will not be walked on and it is not really useable space, where heavy boxes or unwanted items will be put.
- Where cables are placed in a roof, always try and follow along a joist or at right angles to the joists.

Flexible rod for fishing cables.

*Cables clipped to ceiling
joist.*

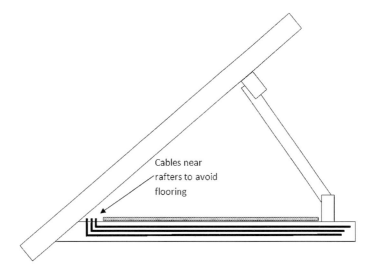

Cables near
rafters to avoid
flooring

Never run the cables diagonally, because if the roof space is to be boarded at a later date, the cables will have to be moved.

Cables in Stud Partitions

It is not unusual for switches and socket outlets to be positioned in stud partitions; access to these is usually quite simple. Where the cable is to enter the stud partition from the top, careful measurement is required to pinpoint the top of the stud wall. If you are lucky, the studwork will have been built before the ceiling board was fixed, in which case you will be able to see the top of the stud easily. When you are relying on measurement, it is a good idea to try and push a small screwdriver through the ceiling board first and see if you can feel the stud below. If you miss, you will only make a small hole in the ceiling, which is far better than drilling a large hole through it.

Once you are sure that you have found the top of the stud, use a wood bit and drill through the stud. When you have drilled the hole, cut a dry wall box into the wall where you want the socket or switch to be put.

Push a fishing tool or a piece of stiff wire down through the hole in the stud until you reach the hole that you have cut. It is now just a matter of fixing a cable to the tool or wire and pulling it up through the wall.

Occasionally you will find that there is a brace running horizontally across the wall. If there is, you will have to measure the position of the brace using

Cut away plasterboard to get past a brace.

the fishing tool or wire. Now you will need to cut a small section of the wall out over the stud and notch the stud to allow the cable to pass over it. When doing this, make sure that the notch is in the correct zone above, below or beside the socket or switch.

Cable Connections under Floors

Where cables are joined under floors, joint boxes must be used and secured in place. This can be achieved by screwing the joint box to the side of the joist or by making a wooden platform to fix the box to.

Where the cables enter the joint box, they should be fixed using cable clips, which will prevent any strain being put onto the cable connections.

The wiring regulations are quite clear that any connections made to cables using screw-type connections must be accessible; this does not mean that we cannot cover the joint box or fix it in to a building void. As long as the joint box can be accessed, even if it involves taking up a carpet, it will not be a problem. The important part, which is more often than not forgotten, is that there must be a record of where the joint box is. A written note with perhaps a plan kept beside the consumer unit is a good idea.

Where a junction box is to be installed in an inaccessible position the regulations state that the connections must be made using a maintenance free accessory manufactured to BS5773 or mechanical crimps. These types of connections can be used for power or lighting cables and unlike screwed connections they will not become loose due to changes in temperature.

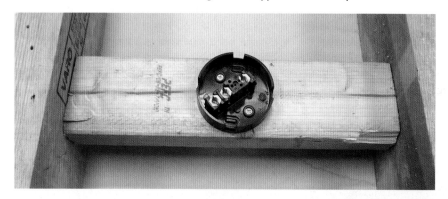

LEFT: Junction box correctly secured.

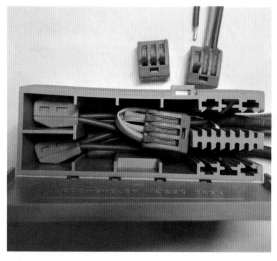

Wago connector.

Crimp connector.

CHAPTER 8

Protective Earthing and Bonding, and Supply Systems

THE IMPORTANCE OF EARTHING AND PROTECTIVE BONDING

Correct earthing and bonding contribute considerably to the safety of almost all electrical installations, and for this reason it is very important that we get it right.

Before we can look at earthing we must understand how a supply system works.

The electricity that we use is generated in power stations using various types of fuel. In the UK, the most common fuels are gas, oil and coal. Electricity is generated at a voltage of 25,000V (25kV). To reduce energy losses, the voltage is increased to a maximum of 400kV and this is known as the transmission voltage.

At this voltage the electricity is delivered all around the country to substations, where it is reduced to 33kV or 11kV for distribution; from the substations it is distributed to supply transformers local to the end user.

From the supply transformer the electricity is delivered to the end user at voltages of 400V or 230V by cables that are either run overhead or buried underground.

To enable us to carry out our installation work and complete our test certificates correctly, we must be able to recognize the difference between

A typical supply transformer.

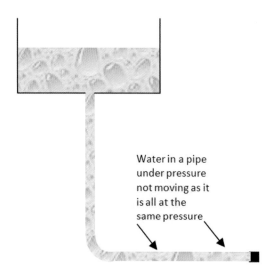

Water in a pipe under pressure not moving as it is all at the same pressure

Water or current cannot flow if there is not a difference in pressure.

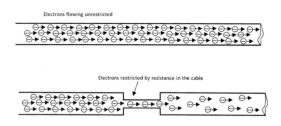

Electrons flowing in a cable.

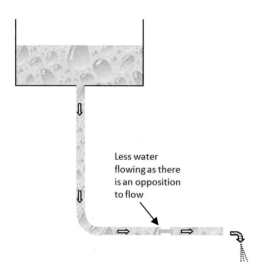

Less water flowing as there is an opposition to flow

Water flowing in a pipe with a restriction.

our supply systems, which are supplying the building in which we are working.

To help us understand, we need to look at how electricity flows through the supply system.

The flow of electricity revolves around three components:

- **Voltage.** This is the pressure at which the electrons flowing through the system are under. It can be related to water in a hose: if you block up one end of a hose and turn on the tap, the water becomes pressurized but does not move. The symbol for this is U.
- **Current.** This is the quantity of electrons flowing in a circuit and it is measured in amperes or amps, as it is more commonly called. This can be related to water flowing in a pipe. The symbol for this is (I). When current is flowing in a circuit all of the electrons flow the same way, just as water would flow the same way.
- **Resistance.** This is the opposition to the flow of current in a cable and is measured in ohms (Ω). Again, this can be related to water flowing in a pipe with a restriction.

It is important for us to understand that to get current to flow, there must be a difference in pressure – again, not unlike water. To provide a difference in pressure, we use the earth.

The current is delivered to us at a voltage of 230V and when we connect a load to the circuit, the current will flow through the load back to the supply transformer. To provide a difference of pressure, an electrode is sunk into the ground, which is connected to the star point of the supply transformer. As the electrical potential of the earth is 0V, we have now created a difference in pressure that will allow the current to flow.

TYPES OF SUPPLY SYSTEM

We have three types of system which are in common use and they are referred to as TT, TN-S and TN-C-S.

TT Supply System

A TT system is normally a supply in which the cables are run into the building above ground. The

Resistance is the opposition to the flow of current.

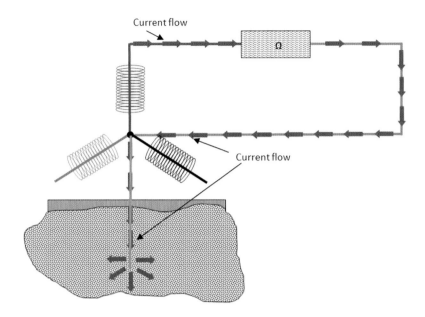

abbreviation TT indicates that the supply system and the installation has two points of earth. The letter T is used because it is the first letter of Terra, which is the Latin word used for earth, dirt or land.

In many rural areas and some urban areas, you will see electricity cables suspended above ground by poles, which look exactly the same as telegraph poles, the difference being that they usually have four wires suspended from them, one above the other.

In most domestic properties two cables are run into the house – these are the line and neutral. In this type of installation, the earth for the property is not supplied by the district network operator (DNO). As it is very important that all installations are earthed, the earth has to be provided locally and becomes the responsibility of the installer.

An overhead supply.

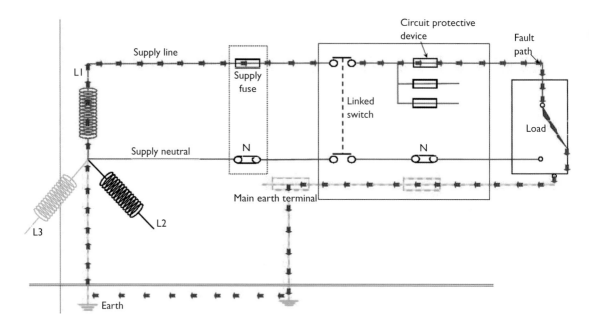

TT earth path.

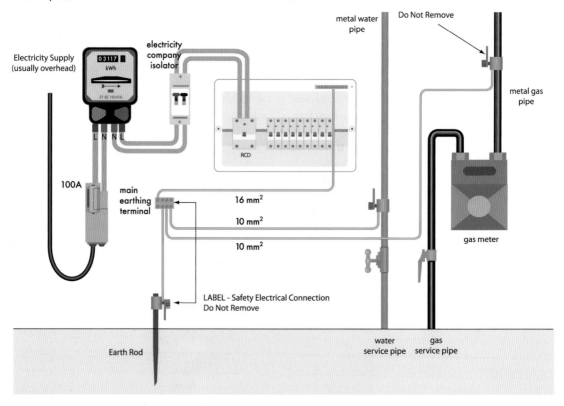

TT service head.

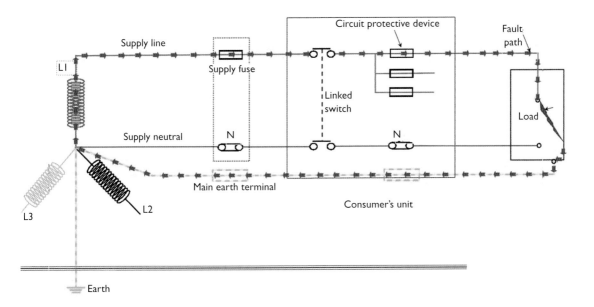

TNS system.

An earth electrode is driven into the ground in a convenient position. An earthing conductor is connected to it and run into the consumer unit; this will provide the earth for the property.

When there is an electrical fault to earth, the fault current will flow through the electrical supply line conductor to the consumer's electrode and then through the earth (soil) back to the supply transformer electrode. The fault current will then flow through the transformer winding to the origin of the supply.

A TT system can usually be identified at the service head; this is because there will be no sign of an earthing conductor being connected to the service head, or the supply cable.

TN-S supply system

A TN-S supply system uses only one point of earth and this is supplied to us by the DNO. The point at which the system is connected to earth is at the supply transformer. In the event of a fault, the current can flow through the sheath of the supply cable or perhaps a separate earthing conductor. The abbreviation TN-S is earth and neutral separate; this is because the earth and the neutral are completely separate throughout the installation.

This type of supply is usually taken into the house underground. The cable is lead-covered and protected by a steel sheath, which is covered in hessian. A connection is made to the lead sheath by the DNO and this provides the earth for the system.

TN-C-S supply system

A TN-C-S system also uses a single point of earth. The difference between this system and the TN-S system is that the supply neutral in a TN-C-S system serves a dual purpose: not only is it used as the neutral conductor, it is also used as the supplier's earth. In this system, the supply neutral is known as the PEN conductor (protective earth and neutral).

In modern houses this type of supply would be run into the house underground. However, there is no reason why it could not be overhead, and in fact many TT systems have been converted to TN-C-S systems. The earthing of this system is provided by connecting an earthing conductor to the supply neutral at the service head. This connection must be made by the DNO and must not be made by anyone else.

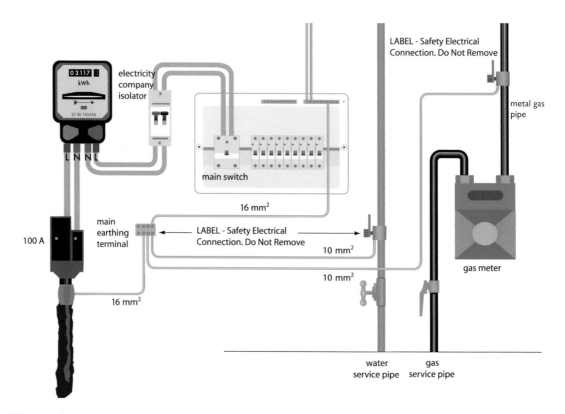

TNS service head.

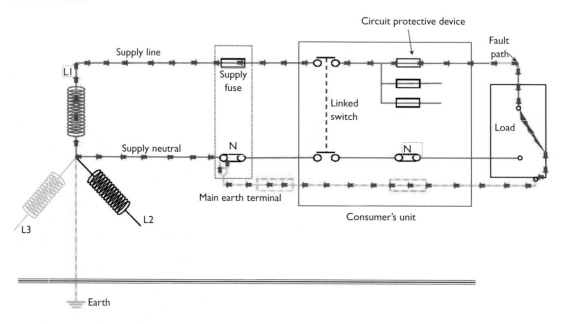

TN-C-S system.

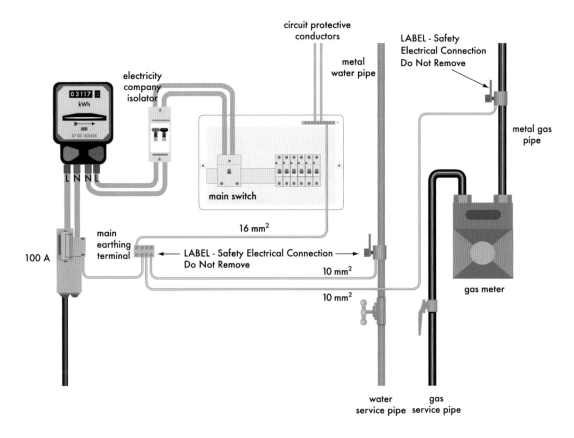

TN-C-S service head.

TN-C-S systems are often referred to as a PME system (protective multiple earthing).

EARTHING

To prevent damage to property, or injury to persons or livestock, when there is a fault to earth it is a requirement that the system is installed so that the supply to the fault is interrupted very quickly. To ensure that this is the case, the supply system and each circuit must be coordinated correctly to ensure that the protective device will operate when required.

This relies on the resistance of the earth fault path being low enough to allow the amount of current to flow that is required to operate the protective device in the required time.

In the first instance, it is necessary to select the correct size of the supply earthing conductor.

Where the system is a TN-S system, the earthing conductor must be a minimum of half the size of the meter tails. For example:

$16mm^2$ tails = $10mm^2$ copper earthing conductor
$25mm^2$ tails = $16mm^2$ copper earthing conductor

For a TN-C-S supply, a $16mm^2$ copper earthing conductor should be used for all installations with meter tails up to, and including, $35mm^2$.

TT systems are dealt with differently because they use an earth electrode and an RCD. The earth fault current will be a lot lower than that which would occur in the other systems.

Providing the earthing conductor is not buried and is protected against corrosion and mechanical damage, it can be $2.5mm^2$. This would require the conductor to be enclosed in mini-trunking or conduit. In cases where the conductor is not protected, it can be 4mm² copper.

In some instances where the earth electrode is a distance from the building, it is necessary for the conductor to be buried in the ground. In these situations the conductor can be 2.5mm², providing it is protected against corrosion and mechanical damage.

Where the conductor is protected against corrosion only, then it must be a minimum of 16mm²; if it is not protected against corrosion, then the minimum size is 25mm².

EARTH ELECTRODES

The most common use of an earth electrode is for providing an earth for a TT system.

A copper-plated steel rod is the most common type of earth electrode for use in a domestic installation; a steel pipe can also be used. Earth plates and underground structural metalwork can also be used where suitable.

Before installing an earth electrode, consideration must be given to where it is going to be positioned. Ideally it should be placed away from areas where it is likely to get damaged or come into contact with chemicals that may cause it to corrode. It must also be in an area where the soil is unlikely to freeze.

An ideal area is one that is in the shade and where the soil has less chance of drying out. A standard rod electrode used in a domestic installation would be driven into the ground to a depth of around 1m. Ideally the electrode will be installed in an inspection pit. In most cases a lightweight plastic enclosure can be used.

Where an earth electrode is used for protection on a TT system, it is important that the electrode provides a low enough resistance to allow enough earth fault current to flow. To operate a 30mA RCD, a fault current of 30mA is required. To allow 30mA to flow through the earth fault path, the resistance of the earth fault loop must be no greater than

$$\frac{50}{0.03} = 1667\Omega$$

Within a TT installation, the touch voltage under fault conditions must never be permitted to rise above 50V. To calculate the maximum resistance of the earth fault loop path, we can use Ohm's law and divide the voltage by the current flow in amperes.

As the trip rating of the RCD used is given as 30mA, we need to divide 30 by 1,000 to convert it to amperes; the maximum permitted earth fault path is 1,667Ω. The problem with using this value is that it will be unstable. Due to the nature of soil, the resistance will change almost daily.

In dry weather the resistance will be higher than it will be in wet weather. If we were to test the resistance of our electrode on a wet day it might have a low enough resistance to make it suitable for use. If the soil were to dry out, as it would in the summer, the resistance would rise, and it might rise above the permitted maximum value.

To ensure that the earthing system remains effective, the maximum resistance of the earth fault loop is limited to 200Ω. Any resistance above this will be considered unstable.

CIRCUIT PROTECTIVE CONDUCTORS

The resistance of the supply side of the installation is something that we have no control over. The symbol for the supply resistance is usually referred to as the external impedance, Z_e. This is because the resistance of an AC circuit is referred to as impedance, and the letter used for impedance is Z.

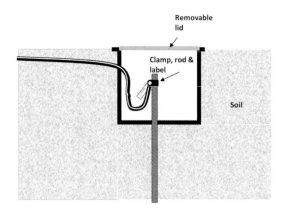

Earth electrode in an inspection pit.

$$Z_e + R_1 + R_2 = Z_s.$$

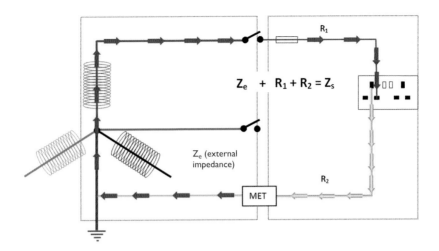

All final circuits that have a current rating of up to, and including, 32A must automatically disconnect from the supply in the event of a fault to earth within 0.4sec. This requires that the impedance (resistance) of the circuit must be low enough to allow the required amount of current to flow. The value of resistance for each circuit is known as Z_s and this is made up of the resistance of Z_e plus the resistance of the circuit line (R_1) and circuit protective conductor (R_2 earth). The formulae used for Z_s is:

$$Z_s = R_1 + R_2$$

As you can see, the value of Z_e is made up of the resistance of the supply line and the resistance of the path that the fault current would take back to the supply transformer; this is known as the earth fault return path. In a TT system, the earth fault path is through the mass of earth; for calculation purposes this is given a value of 21Ω, although in reality it could be anything as the true resistance will depend on the type and size of the earth electrode used, along with the type of soil and the soil condition, which will depend on the weather.

A TN-S system, which uses the metallic sheath of the supply cable, will have a maximum Z_e value of 0.8Ω and a TN-C-S system will have a maximum Z_e value of 0.35Ω.

To ensure that enough current can flow to operate the protective devices, the circuit cables that we install must be very carefully calculated to prevent the Z_s value from exceeding the permitted value.

Tables are provided that show the maximum permitted value of Z_s for the type and rating of the protective device that is being used. It is up to us to use the correct size of cable to ensure that these values are not exceeded. Circuits that are installed with a Z_s value that is too high, could result in electric shock, fire or cable damage.

BS 3036 Semi-Enclosed Rewirable Fuse

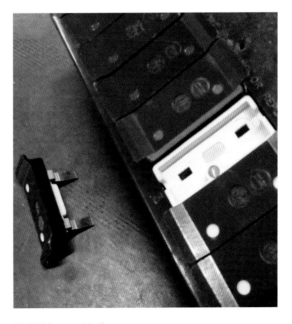

BS 3036 rewirable fuse.

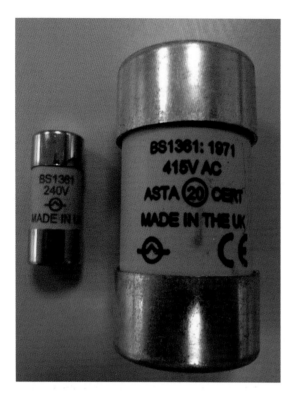

BS 88 cartridge fuse and BS 1361 cartridge fuse.

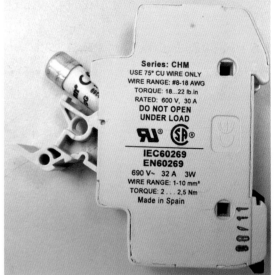

Cartridge fuse carrier.

Maximum Zs value for BS 3036 fuses that must not be exceeded

Rewirable fuses to BS 3036				
Fuse rating	5A	15A	20A	30A
Max Z_s	7.3Ω	1.9Ω	1.3Ω	0.83Ω

BS 88 cartridge fuses and BS 1361 cartridge fuse
Maximum Z_s values for a circuit protected by a BS 88-3 cartridge fuse

Cartridge fuses to BS 88-3				
Fuse rating	5A	15A	20A	30A
Max Zs	7.9Ω	1.84Ω	1.55Ω	0.73Ω

Maximum Z_s values for a circuit protected by a BS 88-2 cartridge fuse

Cartridge fuses to BS 88-2						
Fuse rating	6A	10A	16A	20A	25A	32A
Max Zs	6.47Ω	3.9Ω	2.06Ω	1.34Ω	1.09Ω	0.79Ω

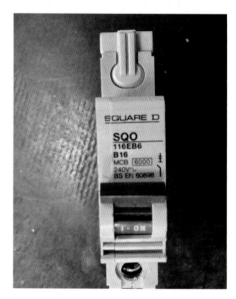

BS EN 60898 circuit breaker.

Maximum Z_s values for a circuit protected by a BS 1361 cartridge fuse

Cartridge fuses to BS 1361				
Fuse rating	5A	15A	20A	30A
Max Zs	8.0Ω	2.5Ω	1.29Ω	0.86Ω

BS EN 60898 circuit breaker

Maximum Z_s values for circuits protected by BS EN 60898 circuit breakers

Circuit breakers to BS EN 60898					
Type	Current rating				
	6A	16A	20A	25A	32A
B	5.87Ω	2.2Ω	1.75Ω	1.4Ω	1.1Ω
C	2.91Ω	1.09Ω	0.87Ω	0.7Ω	0.55Ω
D	1.46Ω	0.55Ω	0.44Ω	0.35Ω	0.28Ω

Let's look at how electric shock could occur if the earth was not correctly connected or the circuit resistance to earth (Z_s) was too high. For example, an electric cooker has become live due to a fault on one of its oven elements and, for some reason, the earthing conductor has not been connected.

In this situation, the case of the cooker will become live, although the elements that have not been damaged will continue to work correctly. If you were to touch the cooker at the same time as you touched the water tap, there is a very good chance that you would receive an electric shock. This is because the tap will be at 0V and the cooker will be at a voltage considerably higher, probably 230V. As there is now a difference in pressure, the current will be able to flow from the cooker, through your body to the tap.

As you can see, earthing is very important, as it is part of the safety system of an installation.

SELECTING THE CORRECT SIZE OF CIRCUIT PROTECTIVE CONDUCTOR

Before we can select the correct size of the cable that we will use, we need to measure the external earth loop impedance Z_e. Measuring this value is covered in Chapter 13. However, we have already seen that we are given maximum values for each system and if we need to, we can use these values for calculation purposes.

Once we know the Z_e value of the system, we need to calculate the resistance of the fault path that the current will take through the cable. This is the $R_1 + R_2$ value for the total length of the cable used. Before we can calculate $R_1 + R_2$ for the total length, we need to know the resistance per metre of the cable. The table overleaf provides us with these values.

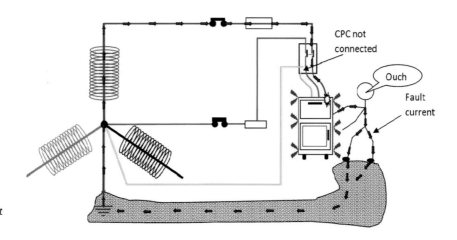

Shock from a cooker that has not been correctly earthed.

Values for resistance per metre.

Cross sectional Area mm²	Resistance mΩ/m
1.0	18.10
1.5	12.10
2.5	7.41
4.0	4.61
6.0	3.08
10.0	1.83
16.0	1.15

The table gives the resistance per metre of copper conductors in mΩ/m when they are at an ambient temperature of 20°C. If the temperature of the conductor were to rise, then the resistance of the conductor would increase; this of course would reduce its current carrying capability.

As an example, let's say we need to install a cable for a new radial socket outlet and the information that we have is:

1. Supply system is a TN-C-S with a Z_e value of 0.35Ω.
2. Circuit protection is a BS EN 60898 circuit breaker 16A type B.
3. The cable that we want to use is 2.5mm² with a 1.5mm² circuit protective conductor.
4. The cable is 17m long.

Using this information, it is quite a simple process to check that the circuit will meet the requirements of BS 7671 with regards to earth fault protection.

Step 1
We must now calculate the resistance for the length of cable. Using the table, we can see that the resistance per metre given for a 2.5mm² copper conductor is 7.41mΩ/m and the resistance of 1.5mm² is 12.1mΩ/m. If we now add them together, we can see that the resistance of our cable is 19.1mΩ/m.

We are going to use 17m of this cable:

$$17 \times 19.51 = 331.7 m\Omega$$

This value is in mΩ and we need to covert it to Ω by dividing it by 1000:

$$\frac{331.7}{1000} = 0.33$$

(we only need to use the first two decimal places). This is the $R_1 + R_2$ value of our cable.

Step 2
Now we can add the $R_1 + R_2$ to the Z_e of our supply to find the total Z_s of our circuit, as:

$$Z_s = Z_e + R_1 + R_2$$

The total Z_s of our circuit is 0.68Ω.

Step 3
We must now refer to the table to see what the maximum permissible value is for our circuit, which is being protected by a 16 A type B circuit breaker.

As we can see, it is 2.2Ω. This is higher than the calculated value for our circuit, which means that it will be suitable.

Z_s in a TT system
You may well be thinking that the previous calculation carried out on a TT system would result in a very high value of Z_s, which of course would be correct. The same cable used for a circuit connected to a TT system would give a Z_s value of:

$$Z_s = Z_e + R_1 + R_2 \ 21\Omega + 0.33 = 21.33\Omega.$$

This value of Z_s would make the use of the circuit unacceptable. This is because, due to the nature of a TT system, it has a high Z_e to begin with.

With TT systems it is normal to have a high Z_s value and for this reason we must use a device called a residual current device (RCD) for protection from earth faults. This device measures the amount of current that is flowing in the line conductor and the neutral conductor.

In a good circuit, the current should be the same in both conductors. When there is a fault to earth, this will result in an imbalance as some of the current will flow in the CPC. When this happens, the RCD will operate and cut off the supply to the circuit.

The use of an RCD for protection is not restricted to TT supplies. In some instances it is very difficult

Imbalance of current in an RCD coil.

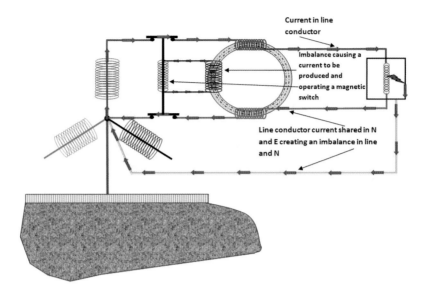

to install a circuit that meets a low enough Z_s value for the circuit protection used on any type of supply. In these instances, it is permitted to use an RCD to ensure a fast disconnection of the supply.

It is important that every effort is made to ensure a low enough $R_1 + R_2$ wherever possible.

PROTECTIVE BONDING

As well as having earthing as protection, we must also have protective bonding. The correct installation of protective bonding considerably reduces the risk of electric shock within an electrical system. As

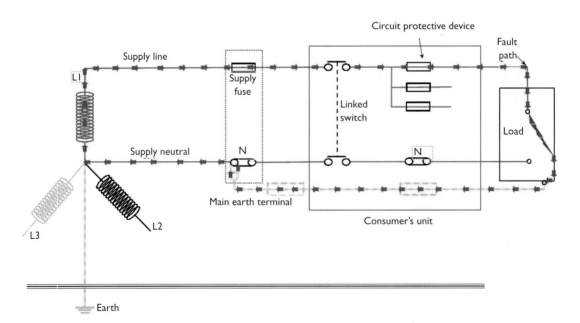

Fault on a piece of class-one equipment in an equipotential zone.

we have seen earlier, there must be an imbalance of pressure for electricity to flow. Protective bonding prevents an imbalance of pressure by joining all metal parts that could become live during a fault.

If the protective device did not operate because the fault current was not high enough, or perhaps the device was faulty or incorrectly installed, then every thing that was connected to the main earth terminal would become live. The correct installation of protective bonding will ensure that there will be no difference in potential between any exposed conductive parts, and extraneous conductive parts within the installation, as it creates an equipotential zone. Everything within this zone will be live, but it will all be at the same potential and in this situation the current will not be able to flow from one live part to another. This will considerably reduce the risk of electric shock.

There are two types of protective bonding: main protective bonding and protective supplementary bonding.

Main Protective Bonding

This is where a conductor is used to connect the main earthing terminal to extraneous conductive parts within the installation. Generally, this would include:

- Metal water service pipes.
- Metal gas installation pipes.
- Oil service pipes installation.
- Exposed structural steel of the building.
- Metal central heating system.
- Air-conditioning system.

Where any kind of bonding is carried out, it is extremely important that it is installed correctly. Always use the correct type of earth clamp to BS 951, which must be fitted in the correct position within the installation.

The connection to the metal services entering the building should be on the consumer's side of the installation, within 600mm of the service meter.

Two types of bonding clamp to BS 951.

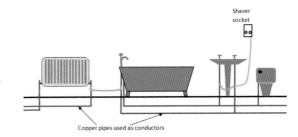

Correct entry into a meter box.

Protective supplementary bonding in a bathroom.

Where the service meter is external, the connection can be made inside the building, as near as possible after the point of entry and before any branch in the pipework. It is also permissible to make the bonding connection in the service meter box outside of the building; in these cases, the cable must enter the box through its own dedicated hole.

Where metal services entering the building are separated from the installation by an insulating section at the point of entry, or are manufactured from an insulating material. The installation pipework may in some cases not require bonding as they may not be extraneous conductive parts.

To see if it is an extraneous part or not, a simple test must be carried out between the possible extraneous part and a known earth. If using a low resistance ohm meter with a $k\Omega$ setting the value above which the pipework will require bonding is 22000Ω. if you test instrument will not measure $k\Omega$ then an insulation resistance tester may be used, and a measured value of above $0.022M\Omega$ would indicate that the installation pipework will require bonding. If in doubt and the installation pipework is metal, then no harm will be done if it is bonded. As a general rule, there is no requirement to bond plastic installation pipes, although in some installations, where large pipes are used and the water has additives such as central heating protection, protective bonding may be installed. This would require the use of metal inserts to attach the earth clamps to.

For TT, TN-S and TN-C-S systems there are calculations that can be made to select the size of main protective bonding conductors. The simplest method is to use $10mm^2$ copper conductors as a minimum. Main protective bonding must have a resistance of 0.05Ω or less. In practical terms this limits the length of a $10mm^2$ copper conductor to 25m; where a length of more than 25m is required, then the size must be increased to 16mm.

Protective Supplementary Bonding

This is used to connect all of the extraneous conductive parts to all of the exposed conductive parts within a building. The use of protective supplementary bonding is often misunderstood. Its function is to ensure that all of the metal parts within a certain area of an installation will rise to the same potential.

When there is an electrical earth fault within an installation, all the metalwork that is connected in some way to the main earthing bar within the consumer's unit will become live. This, of course, includes any class 1 equipment that is plugged in, or connected, to the installation in some way. In most cases the fault will operate the protective device instantly and there will not be a problem. However, if for some reason the protective device does not operate, not only will all of the metalwork connected to the earth terminal become live, any metalwork that is touching the earthed metalwork will also become live. This could include steel baths and bath taps, radiators, pipework and in fact anything metal. Where they do become live, it is likely that they will become live at a different potential; this could present a high level of shock risk, particularly in a room containing a bath or a shower.

To reduce the risk of electric shock, protective supplementary bonding is installed. When installed correctly, the supplementary bonding will ensure

Airing cupboard correctly bonded.

that the potential on all bonded metalwork will be the same, which of course will prevent any current flowing through a person who happens to touch two parts at the same time.

Differences between Main Protective Bonding and Supplementary Protective Bonding

Main protective bonding is used to join all extraneous conductive parts within a building, such as the water and gas installation, to the main earthing terminal. Protective supplementary bonding is used to connect all exposed and extraneous conductive parts within an area such as the bathroom. It is not necessary to connect this bonding conductor to the main earthing terminal, just the exposed and extraneous conductive parts together.

Where bonding is installed, it is a requirement that all connections are made using the correct type of earth clamps to BS 951, and of course that the correct size of bonding conductor is used. Where the conductor is protected against mechanical damage by installing it in mini-trunking or conduit, the minimum size is 2.5mm². For a conductor that is clipped direct or run under flooring, then the minimum size is 4mm². In most instances it is easier and cheaper to use 4mm².

The conductor used for all types of bonding must be identified by using green and yellow coloured cables, just as you would for earthing conductors. Where the bonding is to be carried out in bathrooms that have copper plumbing, the pipework can be used as a conductor, where required. This is very helpful as the pipes will only need to be bonded together at the taps on the basin and bath, and there will no longer be a requirement to run cables to connect the bath, basin or any other plumbed-in equipment as the pipework will ensure electrical continuity elsewhere.

Bonding conductors must also be run from pipework into any electrical points within the area being bonded. Remembering that the pipes can be used as bonding conductors; there is no problem with connecting from an electrical point to a pipe in the roof, as long as the pipe is connected to those being bonded.

Where you can be sure that the plumbing is all copper, the bonding can be carried out in the airing cupboard simply by connecting a bonding conductor to each pipe.

In buildings that have plastic plumbing, or have RCD protection for all circuits in the bathroom, it is unlikely that bonding will be required.

CHAPTER 9

Wiring of Lighting Circuits

Before embarking on the installation of a domestic lighting circuit it must be remembered that the circuit must have what is described as additional protection. This means that the circuit must be protected by a 30mA rcd, as well as overcurrent, short circuit and earth fault protection.

For this type of protection an rcd main switch or an rcbo may be used. The first thing to consider is the conductor size. For lighting, a minimum CSA of 1mm² is required. However, this is a minimum size and, although it is perfectly acceptable, 1.5mm² can be used if preferred. The protective device for this type of domestic circuit will be either a 5A BS 3036 rewirable fuse or a 6A BN EN 60898 circuit breaker.

It is as important that any type of circuit is not overloaded, and in most cases it is good practice not to have more than ten outlets on a domestic lighting circuit. Always remember that one single outlet may supply a number of lamps. It is not uncommon for a centre light to have three or four lamps on it and the same applies to wall lights. In some cases a lighting circuit with ten outlets may well supply fifteen to twenty lamps. Once the circuit is completed, we have no control over the rating of the lamps that can be fitted. Every lighting circuit must be installed with additional protection

ONE-WAY SWITCHING

Most domestic lighting circuits use a wiring system that is referred to as a three-plate loop-in system. In this type of circuit the line and neutral are looped in and out of each lighting point, and a switch line and switch return is taken from each lighting point to a switch position. This is known as a three-plate system.

The connections are then made inside a three-plate ceiling rose or batten holder:

- The brown conductors are all joined together by inserting each one into the centre terminal of the ceiling rose.

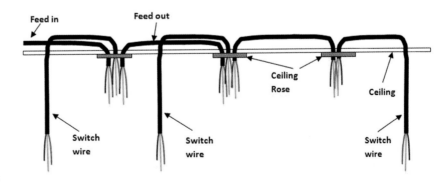

Three-plate wiring system.

- The blue conductor, which is the return from the switch, must have a small piece of brown sleeving placed over it, to identify it as a line conductor and prevent it from being mistaken for a neutral conductor.
- The switch return is then connected to the terminal.
- The blue conductors are then connected to the remaining terminal.
- The CPCs are sleeved and connected to the earth terminal.

The connections are the same for each ceiling rose until you get to the last one on the circuit. At this lighting point there will only be two cables: a feed-in and a switch wire. The connections to be made at this point are:

- The two brown cables (line) are connected to the loop in terminal of the ceiling rose.
- The blue of the live feed is connected to an outer terminal.
- The blue of the switch wire (switch return) must have a brown sleeve placed over part of it for identification and connected into the other outer terminal.

WIRING THROUGH A SWITCH

Another method of wiring, particularly where it is impractical to have a number of cables at an outlet, is to run a live feed to the switch position. In normal three-plate loop-in wiring systems there will

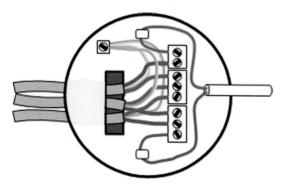

Three-plate ceiling rose connections.

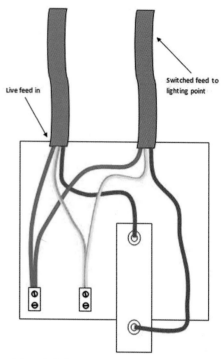

Live feed in

Switched feed to lighting point

Feeds run into switch first.

not be a neutral at the switches; this prevents any light points being wired from the switch.

In installations where the feed is run in and out of the switches instead of the lighting point, connections can be made behind the switch. These connections are very similar to those made in a ceiling rose:

- The brown conductors of the live feed in and out are connected to one of the switch terminals.
- The brown conductor to the lighting point is connected to the other switch terminal.
- The blue conductors are joined using a suitable connection, such as a block connector.
- The CPCs are sleeved and connected to the earth terminal on the mounting box.

In some situations it is not very practical to have more than one cable at a lighting point, as there may not be enough space behind the fitting to make all of the connections. A typical example of this would be a wall light point. Making the connections in the switch is a good way of overcoming this problem.

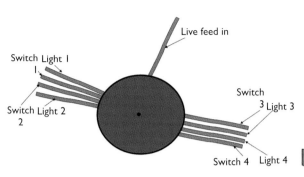

Lighting circuit using a junction box.

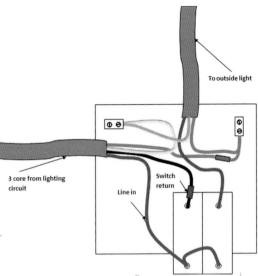

Three-core cable run to switch for neutral.

JUNCTION BOX METHOD

For some installations it may be suitable to use a junction box system. This method requires all of the cables to be run back to junction boxes, which are suitably placed, and all of the connections for the circuit made in the box. The advantages are that all of the lighting points will have only one cable to connect to the light fittings and also the switching of the lighting points can be altered quite simply.

The disadvantage is that often the junction boxes are under the floor and will require carpets to be lifted if alterations are to be made. In a standard three-plate system, the connections can be accessed simply by removing the ceiling rose cover or the light fitting.

Of course there is no reason why a circuit cannot utilize all of these methods. It is not unusual for a circuit that is mainly three-plate at the ceiling light points to have a neutral fed into a switch position. This is particularly useful where an outside light is going to be installed.

A neutral can be provided at the switch point by using a three-core cable as a switch wire and using the third core as the neutral.

ADDING A LIGHTING POINT TO BE SWITCHED ON WITH AN EXISTING POINT

Where an additional light point is required that is to be switched on along with an existing light, a cable must be run from the existing point to the position of the new point. At the existing lighting point the new cables should be connected with the brown conductor to the switch return terminal and blue conductor to the neutral terminal.

Where an additional light is required but with its own switch, then the process is entirely different, as the new switch or the lighting point will need to have a live feed taken to it and then connected using the three-plate or switch method.

TWO-WAY SWITCHING

It is not always convenient to have only one switch controlling a light; for example, in a dwelling that has stairs and the landing/hall light needs to be switched at the bottom and the top of the stairs. This type of switch circuit is known as two-way switching.

The circuit diagram overleaf shows how it works.

A junction box system used in this type of circuit would be fine. The permanent live is fed into the common of one switch, and the switched return is taken from the common of the other switch. This type of wiring is fine for a junction box system or a conduit system where single core cables are used, but it is not very practical for use in a three-plate system.

Where the system is a three-plate loop-in system, the most common type of two-way wiring circuit used is an extended two-way circuit. In this type of circuit, all that is required is for a three-core

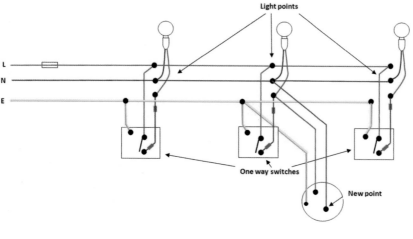

Light points

LEFT AND BELOW LEFT: Adding an extra light on the same switch.

One way switches

New point

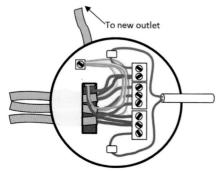

To new outlet

Line in   Switched line out

Lamp

2 Way switches

Strappers

Conventional two-way switching circuit.

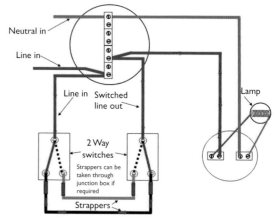

Neutral in

Line in

Line in   Switched line out

Lamp

2 Way switches

Strappers can be taken through junction box if required

Strappers

One-way circuit converted to two-way using a junction box.

cable to be run from the one-way switching position to the second switch position.

The standard colours of the cores in a three-core cable are brown, black and grey. As they are all to be used as line conductors, they must have a small piece of brown sleeving placed over them to identify them. When all of the cables have been installed and the outer sheathing removed, one switch should have two brown conductors and one each of blue, black and grey. The second switch will have one each of brown, black and grey. Both switches should have two bare CPCs, which will need to be covered completely with green and yellow earth sleeving.

When making the connections, the colours used are for identification only. Providing the conductors are connected in the terminals as shown, the colours are not important.

The switches required will be two-way switches and will have three terminals, which will be identified as, common, L1 and L2, or one-way and two-way.

At switch one with five line conductors connect:

- Two browns into terminal L1or one-way.
- Black and blue into terminal L2 or two-way.
- Grey into common.

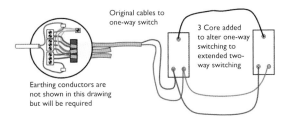

Original cables to
one-way switch

3 Core added
to alter one-way
switching to
extended two-
way switching

Earthing conductors are
not shown in this drawing
but will be required

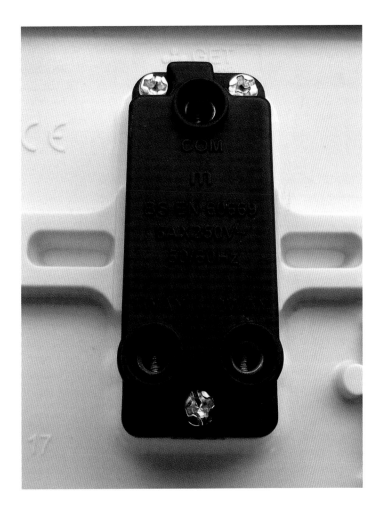

ABOVE LEFT: Extended two-way wiring circuit.

ABOVE RIGHT: Connections at switch 1.

RIGHT: Two-way switch.

Connections at switch 2.

At switch two with three line conductors connect:

- Brown to L1 or one-way.
- Black to L2 or two-way.
- Grey into common.

The CPCs must be joined and terminated in the earthing terminal of the mounting box. If there is not a terminal provided, then the earthing conductors must be connected in to a suitable connector, such as a block connector.

INTERMEDIATE SWITCHING

Intermediate switching is the term given to a system where the same light or lights can be switched on and off from a number of positions.

As with the two-way system, the circuit is fine for a junction box system but not practical for use with a three-plate system. A much simpler method is to use the same method as an extended two-way system and add switches, as required, by looping the three-core cable in and out of the additional switches.

At switch one there will be a switch line and return from the light and a three-core which will go to switch two.

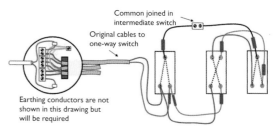

Intermediate switch circuit.

Switch two will have one three-core in and one three-core out; this will be the same for all of the switches apart from the final switch, which will only have one three-core.

The first and last switch will be two-way switches with three terminals. The other switches will be intermediate switches, which will have four terminals marked.

The connections at the switches are as follows (all conductors to have brown identification).

Switch one:

- Two brown conductors into terminal L1.
- Black and blue conductors into terminal L2.
- Grey conductor into the common.

At switch two and all other intermediate switches:

- Grey conductors to be joined and terminated into a connector.
- Brown and black conductor of one cable terminated in L1 and one in L2 on top or bottom of the switch.
- Brown and black conductor of the other cable terminated to the remaining L1 and L2.

It is very important that the conductors of each cable are terminated at the same end of the switch (top or bottom).

At the final switch:

- Grey terminated into the common terminal.
- Brown terminated into L1.
- Black terminated into L2.

LEFT AND ABOVE: Intermediate switch.

Providing all of the connections are made correctly, the light/s can be controlled from any switch position.

WIRING A NEW LIGHTING CIRCUIT

Before starting to wire any circuit it is always a good idea to spend some time thinking the job through first. Things to consider are:

- How many lighting points are there to be on the circuit? (Max. of ten is good practice).
- What size cable is to be used? 1mm² is suitable.
- What type of protection will be required? This would usually be a 6A circuit breaker in a new building but, if the circuit is an additional circuit in an existing building, it is possible that the consumer's unit may contain cartridge fuses or rewirable fuses.
- Will RCD protection be required? In most domestic installations RCD protection will be required, unless the cables are to be clipped on the surface. This is because it is unlikely that, if the

cables are to be buried in the wall, they will be protected by earthed metalwork, or buried to a depth of 50mm or greater.
- Is the circuit going to supply an outlet in a room containing a bath or a shower? If it is, then 30mA RCD protection must be provided.
- Which route will the cables take?
- Is the circuit to be a three-plate loop-in system or will a junction box method be more suitable? A mixture of both will be perfectly acceptable.

Where the new circuit is a rewired existing circuit:

- Are the existing points in the correct position?
- Will it be possible to use the existing switch drop conduits for the new circuit?
- Are the switch boxes suitable? Some older installations have wooden switch boxes, which are no longer suitable for use as they do not comply with the wiring regulations. They will need to be changed for metal or plastic boxes.
- If the cables are to be run under the floor, what type of flooring has been used?
- Will it be possible to lift the flooring to provide access to the cable route without causing damage?
- Will it be possible to provide a suitable fixing at the lighting point position? It is a requirement

of the wiring regulations that the fixing must be capable of supporting a mass of 5kg.

Having decided on the route, if a three-plate loop-in system is to be used, a twin and earth cable must be run from the consumer's unit and looped in and out of each lighting point. From each lighting point, a twin and earth cable must be run to the required switch position.

This sounds very easy and, for a new installation, it is, but of course for a circuit that is being rewired, the installation of the cables is often difficult. It is a good idea to have a look around to see if any floorboards have been lifted previously. In older houses there will probably be quite a few, particularly where the building has had central heating installed after it was built.

Always try to use the existing holes that have been drilled through the joists. If additional holes are required, be very careful not to weaken the joist. Never drill a hole below a notch or another hole.

It is also very important to ensure that cables do not come into contact with hot pipes, as the heat from the pipes will damage the cable over a period of time.

Where the new cable is being pulled through a hole that already has other cables in it, always make sure that the cable is flat, and never pull the cable through the hole quickly, as it will damage the cable that it is being installed next to. Because the cables are PVC, the friction caused by one cable rubbing against another will melt the cable insulation. Often this damage is difficult to see. If the cables are installed carefully, damage will not occur.

Where the cables are to be run through a gap between the floor and the ceiling, it is useful to try and use one of the cables that is being replaced as a draw wire. Where this is not possible, a purpose-made fish rod can be used.

If you do not have a fish rod, any flexible tube can be used – a length of plastic conduit with a small diameter is a good substitute and does the job very well.

For cables that are being run to the switch position, the existing conduit will often be suitable. The problem that normally arises when carrying out a rewire is that additional points are required, which may result in more cables being needed at the switch and the existing switch drop not being large enough to contain them.

Before starting to chase out the wall to install a larger conduit, it is always a good idea to consider the use of a junction box.

As an example, let's look at a room with four lighting points that need to be switched individually. A conventional three-plate system will result in four twin and earth cables being at the switch; this would be four line conductors and four switch returns (one for each light).

There are various methods we could use to reduce the number of wires at the switch, the most basic method being to use a junction box. All that would be required is for the switch cables to be run to a junction box position, and then a three-core and earth cable along with a two-core and earth cable run to the switch. This would give you five conductors at the switch along with two CPCs.

At the junction box, join all of the brown conductors from the lighting points, together with the brown from the two-core cable from the switch into one terminal. This will leave four blue conductors, which are the switch returns to the lighting points – a brown, black and grey from the three-core going to the switch, and the blue from the two-core going to the switch.

In other words, there will be four conductors from the switch and four switch wires from the lighting points.

All of these conductors must have a small piece of brown sleeving placed over them to indicate that they are line conductors.

In the junction box join one of the switch lines from one light to any of the wires going to the switch; repeat this for all four switch lines.

Sleeve all of the CPCs and connect them all into the same terminal in the junction box. All of the cables at the junction box should now be terminated; if they are not, you have done something wrong.

At the switch position we will need a four-gang switch. Loop a brown conductor between all of the terminals marked common.

Connect the brown from the switch to any of the terminals marked common.

Three-plate using a junction box.

Now connect the remaining four conductors, one to each terminal marked one-way. Remember to identify each of them with brown sleeving. Finally, sleeve each of the CPCs and connect them to the earth terminal in the box.

At the ceiling roses, connect the brown cable to the switch line, the blue to the neutral and then connect the earth to the earthing terminal, after sleeving it, of course.

On completion the circuit will have to be tested and the correct documentation completed; this process is explained the inspecting and testing section.

Four-gang switch with looped common.

INSTALLING A DIMMER SWITCH

In most situations the installation of a dimmer switch is a very simple job, providing some thought is given to it before starting.

Is the lamp that is going to be controlled by the dimmer suitable? Some lamps will require a special type of dimmer switch. As an example, a fluorescent lamp cannot be dimmed with a standard dimmer, and if you are going to dim extra-low voltage lights, the transformer used will need to be a suitable type.

Always ask the supplier and read the instructions very carefully before installing anything, as once it is out of its box you will be unable to return it.

Ensure that the power rating of the dimmer is correct for the lamp or lamps to be dimmed. A dimmer with too large a power rating will often cause the lamps to flicker. Too small a power rating will cause the dimmer to overheat and burn out.

Line from joint box connected.

Completed four-way switch.

If the dimmer has a metal face plate, remember that it must be earthed using an earth tail.

In most cases it is simply a matter of isolating the circuit, disconnecting the existing switch and connecting the dimmer switch as shown.

Make sure that the box to which the dimmer is going to be fitted is deep enough for the dimmer to fit into. If it is not, then a new, deeper box will need to be installed. This is just a matter of carefully cutting the old box out and replacing it with a deeper one.

In most cases the existing box will be plastered in to the wall – to remove it without causing damage to the decoration is usually a matter of sacrificing the box. Simply use a small chisel to bend the box inwards on all sides, then using a pair of pliers, grip the box and wiggle it until it comes loose. Once the box has been removed, carefully cut away the wall until it is deep enough to fit the new deeper box into. Remember that the switch will overlap the box by 4 or 5mm, so a little bit of damage to the edges of the hole will be hidden once the switch plate has been fitted. The new box can be fixed by using a plug and screw; this is providing that the wall is thick enough to drill to a suitable depth without drilling right through it. If in doubt it is often better to fix the box back using finishing plaster or bonding plaster; all that is required is for some plaster to be mixed to a fairly wet consistency. A small amount of plaster should then be placed into the hole that has been made for the box to fit into. Be

sure to wet the wall first; this will ensure that the plaster does not dry out too quickly. The box can now be pushed into the hole and any plaster that squeezes out can be cleaned off. Leave the plaster to set and you will find that the box is very secure. Sand and cement can be used for this but it will take longer to set. It is very important that the plaster or sand and cement is left long enough to set properly, preferably overnight. If you try and work on the box too soon, it will come loose and you will have to start again.

INSTALLING A RECESSED LIGHT FITTING

In some installations, recessed light fittings are used and installed into the ceiling. Often these are extra-low voltage but of course this is not always the case. Before recessed lights are installed, consideration must be given to the building regulations, as these may have an effect on the type of fittings being used. Ceilings often form a fire barrier or an acoustic barrier and the fittings that are installed in this type of ceiling must not compromise the performance of the ceiling. In most cases it is better

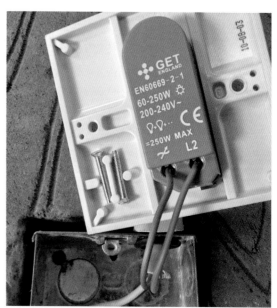

One-way switch connected.

Dimmer connected.

Fire-rated recessed fitting.

to use fire-rated fittings, as these are constructed using intumescent materials, which will prevent the spread of fire; this type of fitting will usually provide an acoustic barrier as well.

If for some reason a fire-rated fitting cannot be used, then a fire hood will have to be installed above the fitting to provide the required fire rating.

Having decided on the type of fitting to be installed, the next step is to ensure that it is possible to fit them where you want them. As the fittings are to be in the ceiling, you will need to identify where the ceiling joists are. If the fittings are on the top floor,

it is just a matter of looking in the roof and taking a few measurements. Unfortunately it is not so easy if the ceiling is fixed to the underside of floor joists. If it is possible to lift a floorboard above the light, then identifying where the hole can be cut is a simple process. On jobs where the lifting of boards is going to be difficult, a joist or stud finder can be used.

It is always best to try and identify which way the joists run first, which can be done by looking at the nails in the floorboards or by tapping the ceiling gently and trying to identify where it sounds hollow. It is also very important to check that there is enough height above the ceiling to accommodate the fitting.

Once you have marked out where the light is to be installed, and you are sure that there are no joists in the way, the hole for the light can be cut.

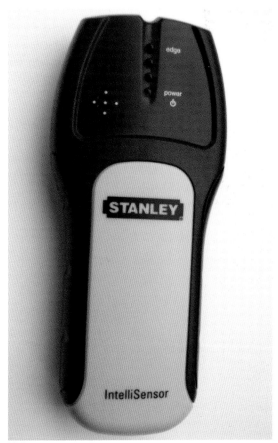

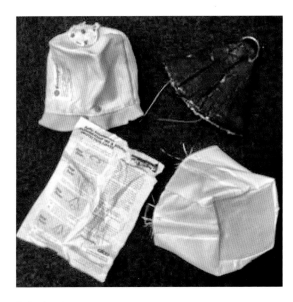

A fire hood.

A stud finder.

A hole saw.

The diameter of the hole will be provided with the light fitting and, in most instances, a template for the hole is provided as part of the packaging.

A hole saw is the best tool to use and is not particularly expensive to purchase.

Where only one or two holes are to be cut, a plasterboard saw can be used. This type of saw is often referred to as a pad saw and special blades can be purchased that will fit into a Stanley knife handle.

When using a plasterboard saw it will be necessary to drill a hole, or possibly two holes side by side, to give the saw blade a starting point.

When cutting around the mark, be careful not to cut through any cables or pipes. If you take your time, you should be able to hear or feel if the blade touches anything other than the ceiling.

Once the hole has been cut, the light fitting can be connected. Some fittings have terminals to which the circuit cables can be directly connected, while others will have a cable to connect to. If the fitting has a cable, the correct method of connection will be by using a junction box. The use of a junction box may also be required if there are too many circuit cables to fit in the light fitting terminals. Where

ABOVE: *A pad saw.*

RIGHT: *Starting point for cutting the hole.*

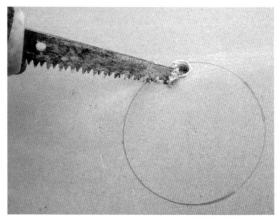

Lighting symbol, suitable to be covered with thermal insulation.

Lighting symbol, not suitable to be covered with thermal insulation.

junction boxes are used it is preferable for them to be fixed to the side of a joist as this will prevent them coming into contact with the lamp fitting.

Most roof spaces will have a layer of thermal insulation, which, of course, will be above the ceiling. In these cases it is very important to ensure that the fitting is not likely to set the insulation on fire or that the build-up of heat will not damage the fitting itself.

Fittings for installation into ceilings will be clearly marked to show whether or not they are suitable to be covered by thermal insulation; those that are will have a symbol to indicate this.

When the fittings are not suitable to be covered by insulation they can still be used but precautions must be taken. They can be covered by purpose-made boxes or shields, which will prevent any problems caused by the heat that the lamps produce.

EXTRA-LOW VOLTAGE LIGHTING

Very often the light fittings used for recessed installations are extra-low voltage. The energy is supplied to this type of fitting by using transformers. A transformer can be used that will supply a number of fittings, or each fitting can have its own dedicated transformer.

Care must be taken when installing extra-low voltage lighting because, although the voltage will be reduced to 50V or less, the current will increase proportionally. The voltage required for most types of extra-low voltage lamps is 12V; this will require the use of a step-down transformer, which in most cases will be a SELV transformer.

A lamp producing an output of 50W that is supplied by a 230V supply will require a current of:

$$\frac{50}{230} = 0.21A$$

A lamp with the same output but supplied by a 12V supply will require a current of:

$$\frac{50}{12} = 4.16A$$

From this calculation you can see that, just because the voltage is low, it does not allow us to use smaller cable sizes and, in fact, it has the opposite effect – we must use larger cables.

In installations where each fitting has its own transformer, it is a simple process to connect the input to the transformer to the 230V circuit. This can normally be by directly connecting to the transformer terminals. In some cases where the light is being installed to a three-plate system, a junction box will be required. The transformer should be fixed close to the light fitting but not so close that it will be affected by the heat produced. Always try and site the transformer close enough to the fitting so that the cables from the fitting do not have to be extended.

The light fitting must be connected to the secondary side of the transformer (output). The cables from the light must be heat resistant and will normally be supplied with the light fitting.

In some installations it may be more practical to use a transformer that is capable of supplying a number of light fittings. Where this type of transformer is used it is very important to make sure that the transformer is sited as close to the centre of the lighting installation as possible. It is important to keep the cable runs to the lights as short as possible. This is because the high current drawn by each lamp will result in a high voltage drop, which in turn will affect the output of the lamp, as a long cable run will result in the lamp operating at a lower voltage and it will not produce the same light output as lamps with a shorter cable length.

Where long cable runs are unavoidable, it is important to check the voltage drop, as it may be necessary to install cables with a larger CSA, which will prevent problems with voltage drop and overloading. Remember, if the voltage drops, the current will rise! In all extra-low voltage lighting installations a cable with at least a cross-sectional area of 1.5mm^2 must be used. A 1.5mm^2 cable that is just over 8m long will result in a voltage drop of 1V; this will reduce the output of the lamp. If the cable length is around 8m, the lamp output will reduce by about 10 per cent. Where a lot of lamps are installed it will be very noticeable if different lengths of cable runs and cable sizes are used.

When using a single transformer for multiple lamp installations it is better to use a larger CSA of cable and to make sure that the cables from the transformer are all the same length.

WIRING AN OUTSIDE LIGHTING POINT

Before attempting to install an outside light, it is very important to ensure that the light fitting that is going to be used is suitable for the environmental conditions that are likely to affect it. In most cases rain will be the biggest concern. Water penetration or corrosion can cause obvious problems, although in some instances dust can also be troublesome. Selecting a fitting with the correct IP rating will prevent problems.

To install a point for an outside light we must consider how the light is going to be switched on. The most basic method is simply to use a switch from inside somewhere. Once the position of the point has been chosen, a sensible route for the cable must be found from the position of the switch to the new outlet. This will require a bit of exploratory work – unfortunately, it is not as simple as just taking a cable from the nearest light switch to the required position, because most lighting switches only have a switch line and return, and do not have a neutral, which will be required for the new light.

For installations where there is a neutral at the switch, it is simply a matter of running a 1mm^2 twin and earth PVC cable from the switch to the light, connecting the light fitting and then the switch. Before attempting to disconnect any cables on or around the switch, carry out the safe isolation procedure to ensure that the conductors that you are going to work on are completely isolated from the supply.

If the light is to be switched individually from the other points that are already wired to the switch, the switch will need to be changed for a two-gang switch or whichever will be required to provide an extra switch.

The procedures for connecting the new point are:

- Decide on where the cable is going to enter the new fitting. If the fitting is going to be exposed to the weather, it is often better to allow the cable to enter the fitting from the back or, if that is not possible, then through the bottom. This, with the correct use of a gland, will ensure that moisture and dust cannot enter the fitting. Of course, the point of entry will also depend on the type of lamp.
- Strip back the mechanical protection from the cable and cut the conductors to the correct length.
- If the conductors are going to come into contact, or be close to, any heat, they must be sleeved with a heat-resistant material.
- Sleeve the CPC with green and yellow earth sleeving and connect it to the earth terminal. If the fitting is class II, then terminate the CPC into a connector.

- Connect the neutral to one side of the lamp or, if the fitting has a connector block, then connect it to N (neutral).
- At this point it is important to carry out a continuity test to ensure that the CPC is not broken. Temporarily connect the brown conductor to the earth terminal at the light fitting.
- Now strip back the mechanical protection from the cable at the switch.
- Using a low-resistance ohm meter, at the switch connect one lead to the new CPC and the other lead to the new switch line.
- Now take a reading. This should be very low, e.g. a 10m length of 1mm² twin and earth cable will

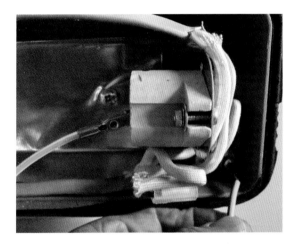

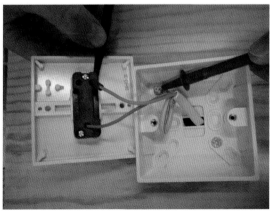

TOP: *Line and neutral connected at light.*

ABOVE: *Using a low-resistance ohm meter to measure resistance.*

have a resistance of 0.36Ω.
- Now part the line and earth at the light fitting and complete the connections to the light fitting but do not put the lamp in yet.
- The test instrument should now be set on MΩ, and an insulation resistance test must be carried out between all of the new conductors at the switch. As this is a new cable, the measured value should be as high as the instrument will read >200MΩ.
- The reason that the cable is tested with all ends parted is to check that the cable is not damaged in any way.
- Now put the lamp in the light fitting and fix any covers.
- At the switch sleeve the CPC with green and yellow sleeving and connect it to the same terminal as the other CPCs. Remember that, if the switch is a metal one, it must have an earth tail connected from the switch to the switch box.
- Identify the live feed-in – this can be done before isolating the circuit. The simplest method would be to turn off all of the lights controlled by the switch.
- Use an approved voltage indicator to test between each terminal and earth or neutral. When the indicator lights up, operate the switch – if the voltage indicator remains on, you must have found the line of the live feed.
- Carefully change the existing switch for the new one with the extra way. Take care that the new switch is connected exactly as the old one was.
- Connect a short length of brown conductor (this can be taken from a piece of twin and earth) between the line of the live feed to the switch and the common of the new switch.
- Connect the brown of the switch wire to the terminal opposite the common terminal and then terminate the blue to the neutral, which will be in a connector of some kind.
- Refix the switch and energize the circuit, operate the switch and make sure that it works correctly.
- If the switch appears to be upside down, isolate the circuit and move the switch wire that goes from the switch to the light to the terminal on the other side of the switch.

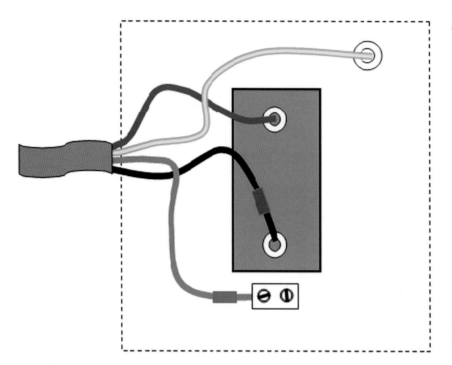

Existing one-way switch.

BELOW: New two-gang switch with neutral in a connector.

- On most switches the terminals for one-way are clearly marked, although sometimes they are not.

Where the lighting point is to be switched alone and a completely new switch position is to be used, the live feed to the new switch can be taken from an existing lighting point, providing of course it has a live feed in it. If the lighting circuit is three-plate it can be checked by unscrewing the ceiling rose cover, and providing the ceiling rose has cables in the centre terminals, it is a safe bet that there will be a live feed there.

Once you have visually identified that there is a live feed, always check by using a voltage indicator. The best method is to test between the centre terminal and the outside terminal with two blue or black wires in it. If the ceiling rose only has two cables, there will be two reds or browns in the centre terminal and a black or blue in each of the outside terminals. One of these black or blue cables will be the neutral, the other is the switched return and should be marked with a red or brown sleeve to indicate that it is a switched return; how-

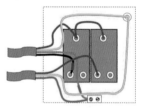

ever, this is not always the case. In these situations, test between the line terminal in the middle, to each of the outside terminals with the blue or black. When the voltage indicator lights, you have found the neutral. Just to be sure, now test from the line conductor to earth and the voltage indicator should light up. Now test between the neutral and earth, and the voltage indicator should not light up.

Now you have found a live feed to connect to you have two options:

- Option 1 is to run a twin and earth cable from the point where the live feed is, to the position at which you are going to install the switch. From the switch you can now run a cable to the light point or points.

Live feed into switch first.

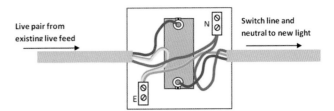

Live pair from
existing live feed

N

Switch line and
neutral to new light

E

Connectors.

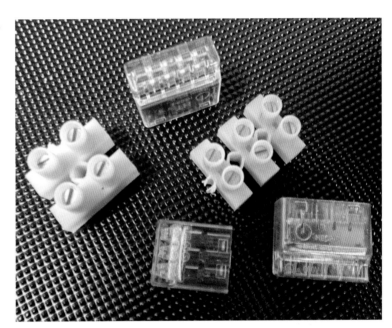

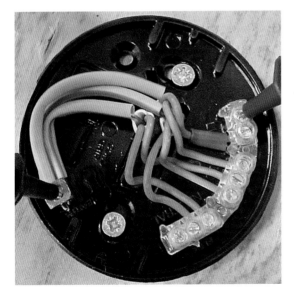

Three plate ceiling rose with permanent line conductors.

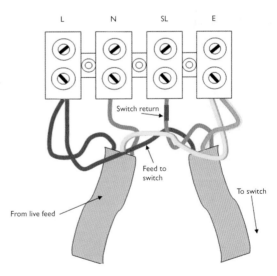

L   N   SL   E

Switch return

Feed to
switch

To switch

From live feed

Connection at the light when live feed run to light.

The switch can now be connected using a block connector or a wago fitting; crimp connections are also acceptable. The light fittings can be connected and the circuit dead tested from the point of the live supply before connecting it.

- Option 2 is to run the cable from the point of the live supply to the light point first and then on to the switch. The problem with this is that you will end up having to make the connections in the light fitting. This can sometimes prove to be difficult with some types of light fittings due to the limited space in them.

Option 1 is the preferred method but in some cases it may not be practical.

WIRING A LIGHTING POINT USING A FUSED CONNECTION UNIT

In some situations it may not be possible to connect your new lighting point to a lighting circuit, or it may be more convenient to take a live feed from a different type of circuit that is easier to access. In these instances, a nicely sited power point could be used. All that is required is for a fused connection unit to be installed next to the power point, and the live feed for the light to be taken from there using the wiring method previously described.

If a power point is unavailable but a cable can be found that conveniently passes near to where you can run a cable to, then it is often useful to cut into the cable using a junction box and then use a fused connection unit as a switch for the light, or to fuse the circuit down and then use a light switch.

OUTSIDE LIGHTS WITH MOTION SENSORS

These sensors are passive infra-red detectors, commonly known as PIRs.

Many exterior light fittings come complete with integral motion sensors. These can usually be fitted in place of an ordinary fitting. In most cases there is no requirement to have a permanent live at the light, and all that is required to set the sensor is to operate the switch on and off, then on again quickly. This operation will set the sensor and the light will operate when someone or something walks within its range.

Passive infra-red detector.

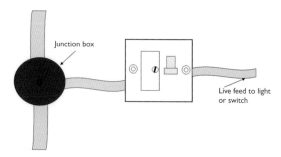

Lighting circuit using a joint box from a power circuit.

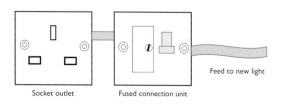

Lighting circuit fused from connection unit.

Some installations will require the fitting of a PIR remote from the actual light fitting; in most instances this will require the use of a permanent live at the PIR.

Using the example of the wiring of an outside light, a three-core and earth cable could be run from the light point to the switch and then onto the PIR

position, or the cable could be run to the PIR first and then a twin and earth taken to the light point from the PIR. Either of these methods would be acceptable among many others that may provide you with different switching options, but remember to identify the line conductors by using brown sleeving.

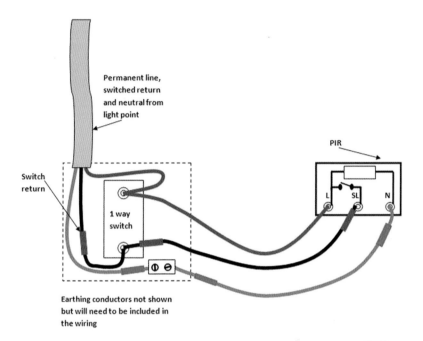

Cable to switch and then PIR.

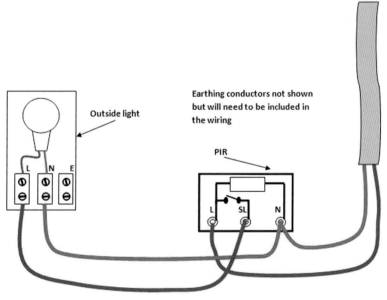

Cable to PIR and then to the switch.

There is one very important thing that must be remembered when testing a circuit with a PIR installed: it must be disconnected before carrying out an insulation test on the circuit. The most important reason is that it could be damaged by the test voltage, the other reason is that it would give a reading of less than 1 MΩ when tested between line and neutral. Where the PIR is remote from the light fitting, it is important to ensure that the cable passing through the PIR is linked or joined together somehow; this is to ensure that all of the cables have been tested.

OTHER METHODS OF SWITCHING OUTSIDE LIGHTS

Outside lighting installations have different requirements, particularly where switching is concerned. Most domestic installations simply require the light to be switched on and off, as required. In some situations it may be that the light is used for security purposes and will be required to switch on when there is movement in the area; in these situations the use of a PIR will be suitable.

There are, however, circumstances when it is

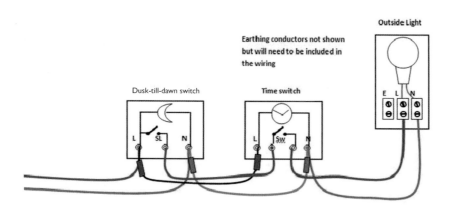

Dusk-till-dawn switch.

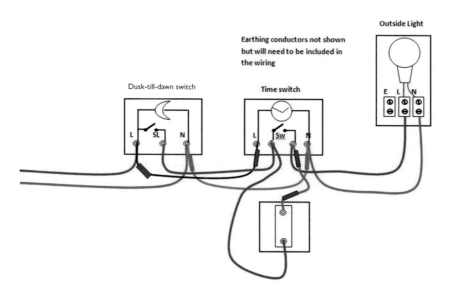

Override switch on dusk-till-dawn circuit.

useful, or even necessary, for the light to be on for a set period of time; this is where a time switch could be used to switch the light on and off at predetermined times. This type of switching is particularly useful where the occupants are working and arrive home in the dark, or perhaps even car-park lighting. The downside of this type of switching is that it can be wasteful, as often the light will be on when it is not dark; this of course is due to the changes in seasons and lighting-up times.

One method of overcoming this is to install a light-sensitive switch. This type of switch will turn the light on at dusk and it will turn it off again at sunrise. This type of switching system is very useful for street lighting or anywhere that requires illuminating at night for security reasons. In domestic situations though, this can also be very wasteful as most people do not need the lights on all night.

One way of overcoming this problem is to use a dusk-till-dawn (light-sensitive) switch and a time switch together. All that is required is for the time switch and the dusk-till-dawn switch to be wired in series.

The time switch would need to be set to switch on around midday and off at the required time at night. This would allow the dusk-till-dawn switch to turn the light on at dusk and then the time switch would switch off at the required time.

The problem with this, of course, is that it could not be switched on if required after the time switch has operated; for this reason it is usual to install a manual override switch or a motion sensor, which switches across the time clock, if required.

WIRING A LOFT LIGHT

It is often useful to have a light point in the loft area. A lot of us are short of storage space and the loft provides a good area to store all manner of bits and pieces. It's fair to say that most of it gets thrown away and we wonder why we stored it in the first place. It always seems a good idea at the time though. Another good reason is to provide lighting for maintenance. Lots of dwellings have tanks and ball valves in the roof area, admittedly all of the time that they give no problems we don't even think about them. When something goes wrong, light is very important as it makes carrying out repairs much easier.

The simplest way to install a loft light is to use one of the methods as explained for wiring an outside light. The cables can be clipped to the surface in the roof and, due to the loading current, loading contact with thermal insulation is not an issue. Be careful not to clip the cables on to the top of surfaces where

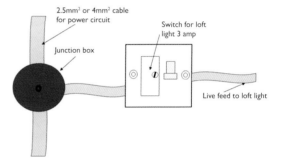

Loft light taken from a power circuit.

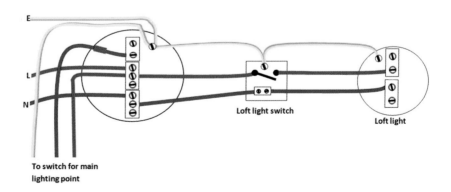

Loft light taken from a lighting circuit.

people may tread when accessing or working in the roof-space area. If the loft light is to be supplied from a lighting point, an ordinary light switch can be used. Where it is to be supplied from a circuit other than a lighting circuit that runs through the roof space, a junction box should be used. A fused connection unit fitted with a 3A fuse should be used as a switch; this will provide protection for the new lighting point.

When connecting into a circuit, it is good practice to use the same size cable as the circuit to which you are connecting to, and then reducing the cable on the outgoing side of the fused connection unit. Although it is good practice, it is not a requirement, and a smaller cable can be used providing it is not more than 3m long. Before it is fused, the cable must also be protected from damage; this can be by putting it in mini-trunking or simply by placing it out of harm's way.

It is a good idea to site the switch outside of the roof space. A simple method it to use a dry wall box and fix the switch into the ceiling next to the loft hatch. The use of a switch with a neon indicator fitted to it, which illuminates when the light is on, is also a good idea; this will help remind the occupier that the light is on and prevent the waste of expensive energy.

LIGHTING CIRCUITS WITH NO EARTH

Until the late 1960s there was no requirement to provide an earth in lighting circuits and most switch boxes were made of wood. Of course this has changed now but there are still very many houses that have not been rewired, and the circuits are as they were when first installed.

The condition of the wiring is usually pretty good as PVC has a very long lifespan. In an ideal world, all of these types of circuits would be re-wired. Unfortunately, although desirable, often for various reasons this is not always possible.

There are no regulations that say the circuits have to be replaced. However, there is a requirement that they remain as safe as possible. Problems usually arise when the circuits require alteration or repair. Of course, any alterations to the circuit will be very limited, as anything that is done will need to comply with the latest edition of the wiring regulations; this rules out extending the circuit or fitting any class-one equipment to it.

The best way to deal with this type of circuit, when it is not possible to rewire, is to make sure that:

- All light fittings are class II.
- All switches are insulated plastic switches.
- All switch boxes are plastic insulated boxes.

This will significantly reduce the risk of electric shock.

CHAPTER 10

Power Circuits

13A SOCKET OUTLETS

Socket outlets can be wired individually or in groups; this is usually dependent on what the outlet is being used for. Most circuits that we install are of the radial type; however, an exception is made for circuits supplying socket outlets.

The most common type of socket outlet circuit in the UK is known as a ring final circuit. In this type of circuit the cable starts at the consumer unit, it then loops from one outlet to another and then back to the consumer unit forming a complete ring of cable.

The benefit of this type of circuit is that smaller cross-sectional area cables can be used. Most commonly this would be 2.5mm^2 live conductors with a 1.5mm CPC. Also, the circuit can accommodate a large number of outlets, and voltage drop around the circuit is normally very low.

The rules for ring final circuits are as follows:

- Maximum protective device size is 32A.
- Maximum area served is 100m^2.
- There is no limit to the number of outlets on a single circuit.
- A ring circuit can have as many socket outlets spurred from it as there are socket outlets on the ring.

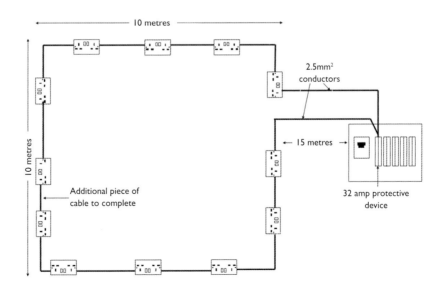

A ring circuit.

- An unlimited number of fused connection units can be spurred from the ring.
- All socket outlets in a domestic environment must have additional protection provided by a 30mA rcd. The only exception to this regulation is that rcds may be omitted in areas other than domestic provided a written risk assessement has been provided which shows that it would be safe not to have rcd protection.
- A spur cannot be taken from a spur.

Wherever possible it is always better to try and include all of the outlets within the ring but on occasion it is useful to spur off the ring, particularly if an additional socket is being added at a later date.

Wiring a ring circuit is a simple process and all that is required is a bit of careful planning before starting the job. First, identify where the socket outlets are going to be sited and plan the route to make sure that it is possible to get the cable to the required position. This should be done before any cutting-in of boxes or chasing of walls is done.

Once you have planned the route, the cable should be looped from one point to another, forming a ring back to the beginning of the circuit; all of the socket outlets can be connected and fixed back. When connecting the sockets, do not twist the conductors together, but enter them separately.

Conductors connected into the correct terminals.

Always sleeve each protective earthing conductor separately and again do not twist the ends together. If a metal socket outlet is being used with a metal box, then make sure there is an earth tail connected between the socket outlet and the box; this is a requirement of the regulations.

When all of the socket outlets have been fixed back, the ring circuit should be tested before the final connection to the consumer unit. The testing process is explained in Chapter 13.

Conductors entered separately.

Once the testing has been completed, the conductors can be connected: both ends of the CPC should be connected into the same terminal of the earth bar; both ends of the neutral conductor should be connected to the corresponding neutral terminal; and, finally, the line conductors should be connected to the 32A protective device. It is important that the line, neutral and CPCs are connected to the corresponding terminals.

The disadvantages of using a ring circuit are that dangers can arise and not be obvious to users; an example would be where one of the conductors on the ring became an open circuit. The circuit would operate normally although the result would be that the cable is vulnerable to overload. The cable would only be capable of carrying a load of 20A but would be protected by a 32A device. Also, the value of the circuit Z_s would increase and the circuit device might not operate in the event of a fault.

This is another good reason why periodic testing of installations is important.

ADDING AN OUTLET TO AN EXISTING RING

As mentioned earlier, it is possible to add more sockets to a ring circuit if required but there are certain rules that have to be followed. When we add a socket to a ring, it is known as a spur. We can spur as many double-socket outlets to a ring as there are sockets on the ring; the socket on the ring can be a single or a twin socket.

When a socket has been spurred from the ring, the cable supplying the socket is the spur and it is known as an unfused spur; the socket is *not* the spur. The spur can be taken from an existing socket outlet or a junction box can be cut into the circuit and the spur can be taken from that.

Under no circumstances should a spur be taken from a socket that is already a spur. A ring circuit is wired in 2.5mm² cable, which can safely carry a load of around 20A minimum; this depends on the installation method. The circuit is protected by a 30 or 32A protective device and the reason that this is permitted is because the circuit is wired as a ring, and the current can flow through the circuit along both legs of it. This, of course, provides a capacity of 40A, which will comply with our regulations, as the cable rating is equal to, or greater than, the rating of the protective device.

When we spur a cable from the ring we must use, in most cases, the same size cable as the ring is wired in. When we spur a 2.5m² cable from the ring, it is a single cable with a minimum current capacity of 20A. This is fine for one twin socket outlet, as even if we load the socket outlet to its capacity, it will not overload the cable; although the cable is rated at less than the protective device, it is permitted.

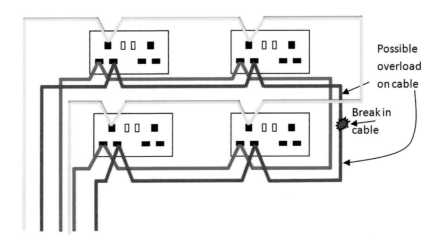

Ring circuit with open circuit.

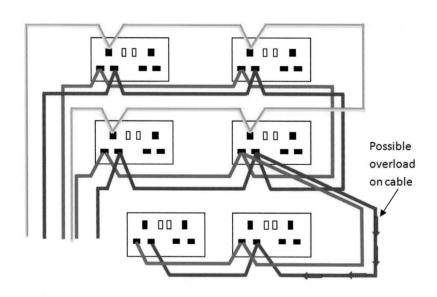

Spur from a spur.

Possible
overload
on cable

The reason for this is that any item of equipment that is plugged into the socket outlet will be fused in the plug top, which will prevent the equipment overloading and, in turn, the cable, as a maximum load of only 26A will be drawn. If a second outlet was spurred from the spurred outlet, a maximum of 52A could be drawn, which of course would result in the overloading of the spur.

Where more than one outlet is required, it is possible to spur from a socket outlet to a fused con-

nection unit first. The cable in this instance would be called a fused spur, as opposed to the unfused spur used for spurring a socket outlet. Once a fused connection unit has been spurred, any number of socket outlets can be taken from the outgoing side of the spur, as the 13A fuse in the connection unit will protect the cable.

Not all equipment has, or even requires, a 13A plug. Very often it is more convenient to permanently connect an item of equipment to a fused

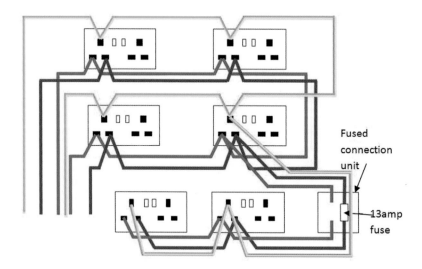

Fused
connection
unit

13amp
fuse

*Sockets spurred from a
fused connection unit.*

connection unit. It is permissible to spur as many fused connection units from a ring as required; there is no limit to the number providing a spur is not taken from a spur.

RADIAL CIRCUITS FOR SOCKET OUTLETS

Another method of installing socket outlets is by using a circuit called a radial. This method is preferred by many installers and designers, as it is not as open to abuse as ring circuits. A radial circuit consists of any number of socket outlets wired by looping a cable from the consumer unit to each socket in turn and terminating at the final outlet on the ring.

The circuit is usually wired in either 4mm² live conductors with a 1.5mm² CPC, or 2.5mm² live conductors with a 1.5mm² CPC.

Circuits wired in 4mm² can be protected by a device rated up to 32A and serve an area of up to 75m²; those wired in 2.5mm² can be protected by a device of up to 20A and serve an area of up to 50m².

The attraction for this type of circuit is that it cannot be compromised by breaks in cables and spurs being installed. In the event of the circuit con-

ductors becoming disconnected or broken, all of the outlets after the break will not work; this is not the case with ring final circuits.

Spurs, either fused or unfused, can be added as and when required. Spurs can be taken from spurs with no risk of overload; this can be clearly seen in the radial diagram.

There is one point worth considering and that is that where the circuit is used in areas where the load is likely to be high, such as a kitchen, it is advisable to use 4mm² live conductors. This is also good advice where ring final circuits are wired in areas with heavy loads.

FUSED CONNECTION UNITS

Fused connection units can be installed and used for various purposes, they can be switched or unswitched, they can also have an integral RCD. Where a fused connection unit is being installed on a ring circuit, there is no limit to the number that can be installed. However, the same rules apply for fused connection units on a ring: it is not permissible to spur from a unit that has already been spurred, unless of course the supply for them is taken from the load side of a spur.

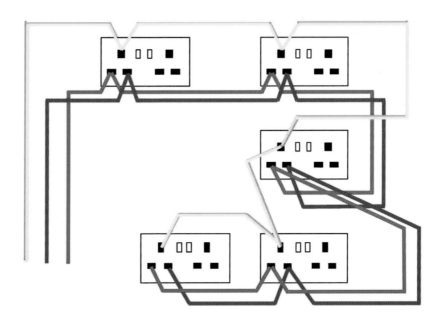

Radial circuit.

ABOVE: Correct connections for a socket after a spurred connection unit.

RIGHT: Unswitched fused connection unit.

Consideration should always be given to what the fused connection is going to be used for, and they must never be used to supply equipment that is rated at greater than 3kW. As with anything else in the electrical world, it is better not to load a fused spur to its capacity, particularly where the load is to be on for long periods.

Where these situations cannot be avoided, it is always a good idea to use a good quality brand of connection unit. Any equipment that is used has to be to a BS or BS EN standard, but this is the minimum standard required; for that reason some manufacturers are better than others.

Very often fused connection units are used above kitchen worktops to provide isolation for socket outlets that are behind washing machines, dish-washers and similar pieces of equipment, where the cord supplying the equipment needs to be hidden.

Where a fused connection unit is to be used for equipment such as alarm panels, it is usual to use an unfused switch spur; this of course will prevent unintentional switching-off of equipment.

If it important to see at a glance whether or not the connection unit is on, a neon-indicated spur can be used. Care must always be taken to ensure that the connection unit is connected correctly with the supply and load, being connected to the correct terminals.

WIRING AN OUTDOOR SOCKET OUTLET

It is often very useful to have access to power out-side, and often we run an extension lead through a window or a door. This is fine as a problem solver but it can be very dangerous. Apart from the obvi-ous tripping hazard, imagine what could happen to the cable if the door slams shut or the widow is closed with the lead still in place.

A socket outlet can be installed on the outside of a property using the same principles as described for the addition for a socket outlet indoors. The best and easiest way is to try and locate a suitable

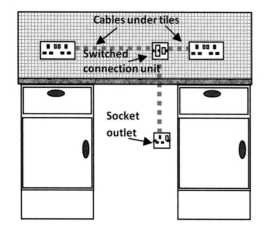

Fused connection unit used as an isolator for a socket outlet.

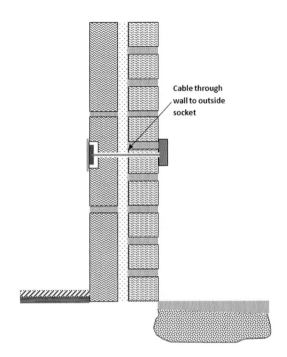

Socket through wall for outside use.

position that is at the back of a socket that is on an outside wall. In these situations it is simply a matter of drilling through the wall to the outside and connecting a cable between the two sockets.

Any socket outlet that is installed must be suitable for the environmental influences that are likely to affect it. For an outside socket, water and dust would usually be the problem and the socket outlet should be rated for IP56.

As with any new socket outlet, additional protection will be required. This will require the fitting of a 30mA RCD. If the building has been rewired or built new since 2008, then the circuit should already be protected by an RCD. If it was wired before then, it may be necessary to use an RCD-protected socket outlet.

Remember also that if the cable is to be buried in the wall, other than passing through from one socket to the other, the cable will require RCD protection. The simplest method of providing RCD protection for the buried cable would be to change the protective device for an RCBO; this will only be possible if the consumer's unit is of the type that accepts circuit breakers. Where the circuit breaker is changed, an electrical installation certificate must be completed and the local building control informed.

Where the circuit breaker cannot be replaced, the new socket can be installed through an RCD-protected fused connection unit fitted next to the outlet that it is being spurred from. This method will not require the socket itself to be the RCD-protected type, it will also only require the completion of a minor works certificate without needing to notify building control.

COOKER POINT

When wiring a cooker point, the same process should be followed as for all other circuits; planning is very important and will save problems and time.

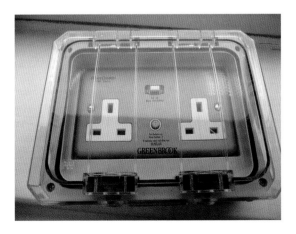

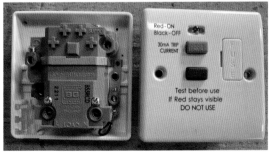

ABOVE: RCD-protected connection unit used for protecting a socket with a buried cable.

LEFT: RCD-protected waterproof socket.

When we are installing a point for a cooker we need to ensure that the cable is a suitable size to carry the current required, as cookers vary greatly in loading.

Calculating the Total Load of a Cooker

As an example, lets take a cooker with the following:

Two hob plates with a maximum output of 1.5kW each = 3kW.
One hob plate with a maximum output of 2kW = 2kW.
One hob plate with a maximum output of 1kW = 1kW.
One oven with a maximum output of 4.5kW = 4.5kW.
One small oven with a maximum output of 2kW = 2kW.
One grill with a maximum output of 2.5kW = 2.5kW.

This will give us a total load of 15kW, which can now be converted to amperes by dividing by the voltage:

$$\frac{15000}{230} = 65.2A$$

This type of load is not unusual for a cooker. However, it is unlikely that in a domestic installation the whole of the load will be on at any one time, even on Christmas Day. This is because all of the elements are controlled by thermostats and different types of food require different cooking times.

Taking all of this into consideration, we can use something called diversity. This is something that will be explained in detail, and a cooker is a good place to start.

Because all of the loads of the cooker will not be on together, we can carry out a simple diversity calculation to take this into account:

From the total load of 65.2A we can use 10A.
This leaves 65.2 – 10 = 55.2A.
Of the current that is left, we can use 30 per cent.
55.2 × 30 per cent = 16.56A.
Now we must add to the 16.65A the 10A that we subtracted.
This gives 26.65A, which is the total load that we need to allow for the cooker circuit. This is why most cooker circuits are rated at 32A and are wired in 6mm² cable.
Some cooker outlets have a 13A socket outlet incorporated in them; in these cases another 5A must be added to the total. In this case 26.65 + 5 = 31.65A, which still allows us to use a 32A protective device.

This calculation can be used for all domestic cooker installations.

First, we must calculate the total load of the cooker; this is often given in the user instructions but if we can't find it we can always calculate it.

It is not unusual for an oven to come pre-fitted with a 13A plug top and the hob to be a separate piece of equipment. In these instances it is desirable to wire a 13A socket from the load side of the cooker outlet, as well as connecting the hob to the cooker outlet.

Where the hob is sited in a different part of the kitchen from the oven, it is acceptable to simply plug the oven directly into the ring and use the cooker outlet for the hob. It is a requirement that the cooker switch is within 2m of the cooker. Where there is a distance between the hob and the oven, using a socket outlet for the oven is a good way of complying, and diversity would only be needed for the hob, which may reduce the cable size even further.

DIVERSITY

In most, if not all, installations, the full load will never be used and for that reason diversity can be applied not only to circuits to help us select the correct cable size, but it can also be applied to whole installations to help us make a realistic assessment of the total amount of energy required from the supply.

It would not be unusual for a dwelling to have the following circuits:

One 32A cooker circuit.
Two 32A ring final circuits.
One 16A immersion heater circuit.
Two 6A lighting circuits.

If added together, the total load could be as much as 124A. If we consider that the maximum rating of a single-phase, domestic supply is 100A, with many of the supplies only 80A or even 60A, we can see that even a small installation will in total exceed the supply. If we were to install a 10kW electric shower, we could add at least another 45A to this and the total demand would be getting close to double the rating of the supply.

This is, of course, where diversity helps us, as when we apply to the district network operator

(DNO) for a supply they will need to be told the maximum demand taking into account diversity. This is because it is fairly obvious that not everything will be used together.

Diversity tables are available to help us but they are only intended as a guide, and even if we use them, the calculated demand in many installations will exceed the rating of the supply.

Using the table lets look at applying diversity to the example we used earlier:

One 32A cooker (diversity already applied to this) = 32A.
One 32A ring final circuit at 100 per cent = 32A.
One 32A ring final circuit at 40 per cent = 12.8A.
One 16A immersion heater 100 per cent 3kW heater = 13A.
Two 6A lighting circuits at 66 per cent = 7.92A.
Total = 97.72A.

Note: where a fixed load, such as an immersion heater, is connected, the actual load can be used.

Using the diversity tables this installation just about scrapes in below the rating of the supply fuse. If we were to add the shower, which was mentioned earlier, the maximum demand will be much higher. In reality the load will be far less than this.

Most domestic ring circuits will never be loaded up to full capacity. The highest load in most houses will come from the kitchen when items of equipment such as the washing machine and dishwasher are used. Most other equipment in a kitchen is possible high-current but will used be used for a short time only. Where a dwelling has central heating, it is unlikely that the immersion heater will be used on a regular basis. It is unlikely that 66 per cent of all lights will be on at the same time. Even if they were, it is extremely unlikely that each circuit will have nine 100W lamps, which is what would be required if the circuit load was to be 4A:

$$\frac{9 \times 100}{230} = 3.91\text{A}$$

When working out the maximum demand, common sense has to be used and we must remember that not everything will be on at the same time. In reality most equipment will only be used intermittently.

It is fair to say that many installations have far more circuits and greater loads that the one used in our example. Ask around and see if you can find anyone whose supply fuse has operated due to overload. It is very unlikely that you will.

Diversity table.

Purpose of the final circuit to which diversity applies	Individual households including individual dwellings in a block	Small shops, stores, offices and small business premises
Lighting	66 per cent of total demand	90 per cent of total demand
Heating and power	100 per cent of total load up to 10A and 50 per cent of the remainder	100 per cent of largest load and 75 per cent of the remainder
Cooking appliances	The first 10A and then 30 per cent of the remaining load + 5A, if a socket outlet is included	100 per cent of the largest + 80 per cent of 2nd largest, then 60 per cent of the remainder
Motors (not lift motors)		100 per cent of largest motor + 80 per cent of the 2nd largest and 60 per cent of the remainder
Instantaneous water heaters (showers)	100 per cent of the first two largest added and 25 per cent of the remainder	100 per cent of the first two largest added and 25 per cent of the remainder
Thermostatic water heaters (Immersion heater)	No diversity	No diversity
Floor heating	No diversity	No diversity
Storage and space heating	No diversity	No diversity
Socket outlet circuits, ring or radial (13A outlet circuits)	100 per cent of largest demand + 40 per cent of remainder	100 per cent of largest demand + 50 per cent of all others
Socket outlets other than those above and any fixed equipment not listed	100 per cent of largest point used + 40 per cent of all others	10 per cent of largest used + 70 per cent of all others

Diversity can be used to calculate maximum demand but realistic values must be used and a great deal of thought should be given to what equipment is likely to be used and when. You cannot simply keep adding circuits, because if you do, overloads can occur and the supply fuse may melt.

INSTALLING AN IMMERSION HEATER

An immersion heater would need to have its own circuit; this is because any water heater that has a storage capacity of greater than 15L must be connected to its own dedicated circuit. Most immersion heaters circuits are wired in 2.5mm² live conductors with a 1.5mm² CPC.

As with all circuits, the route that the cable is going to run, wherever possible, should avoid thermal insulation and be kept as short as possible. If the cable is going to be buried in a wall or run through a stud partition, it must be either installed in an earthed enclosure or protected by a 30mA RCD. A cable with an earthed sheath, such as FP 200 gold or SWA, can also be used, although the simplest method for most installations is to use an RCD.

The circuit must be protected by the correct rating of protective device. Usually, a new circuit would be protected by a 16A type B BS EN 60898, although fuses can be used if desired. The cable should be terminated locally to the immersion heater and provided with its own dedicated switch.

Bearing in mind that the heater will draw a current of 13A, I always prefer to use a 20A double pole switch rather than a fused connection unit, which, when on, will be operating at its full load. I have lost count of the fused connection units that I have had to change over the years due to overheating, mostly on circuits that are used regularly.

Smaller cables can be used, and where they are, calculations must be carried out to ensure that the method of installation, voltage drop and maximum

Immersion with stat and cut out.

Z_s values are all taken into account. Cable calculation is dealt with in detail in Chapter 11.

Once the circuit has been installed, the immersion heater will need to be connected. The cable used for this will usually be butyl rubber cable 1.5mm². Before attempting to connect the immersion heater, make sure that the circuit that it is being connected to has been safely isolated.

The immersion heater will have a thermostat, which must be connected and set to 60°C. The immersion heater must also have an integral temperature limit switch, which can only be reset manually. This switch will ensure that if the thermostat fails, the immersion heater does not boil.

INSTALLING AN ELECTRIC SHOWER

Electric showers are instantaneous water heaters with a shower hose attached. When switched on, the water passes through a small cylinder that has a heating element inside it.

To ensure that the shower has a good flow rate, the element has to provide enough energy to heat the water quickly; this is why most electric showers have a high current rating.

A shower rated at 9.5kW will draw a current of:

$$\frac{9500}{230} = 41.3A$$

This is a large load to be placed onto a domestic supply, which as a maximum will have a current rating of 100A. As we have seen, diversity helps us out in most cases, but unfortunately the guidance given in various documents tells us that diversity should not be used for instantaneous water heaters. Of course this does not prevent us from installing one, if required; however, before we do, we must ensure that the existing installation is not fully loaded before we start.

Consideration should be given to the loads that are already connected. A commonsense approach is all that is required, just to check that it is unlikely that lots of heavy loads are not going to be used together for a prolonged period. We must also bear in mind that the shower is only likely to be used for short periods.

Providing the installation does not have a history of the main fuse blowing, and the main supply fuse is 100A, in most cases the addition of a shower circuit will not have a detrimental effect.

The correct size cable must be used. Most manufacturers' instructions will recommend the cable size for a particular shower. BS 7671 wiring regulations state:

> Electrical equipment shall be installed in accordance with the instructions provided by the manufacturer of the equipment.

This regulation effectively prevents us from using smaller cables, although in most cases calculations could be used to prove that the cables recommended are oversized.

Using the manufacturers' instructions for a 9.5kW shower, a 10mm² cable is required.

Having checked that the supply is suitable for the additional load, we need to check that the consumer's unit has a spare way for the shower circuit. Providing there is space, a suitable protective device can be installed. The current rating of the device (I_n) must be equal to, or greater than, the current rating of the shower. It is also worth remembering that any circuit in a room containing a bath or a shower must be protected by a 30mA RCD.

We must also ensure that the shower has suitable isolation; this can be a cord switch or a wall-mounted switch, whichever is the most suitable. The isolator used must be correctly rated and double pole to ensure that when isolated, both live conductors will be isolated.

The switch must be situated outside of zones 0 and 1. This means that if it is a wall switch, it must be at least 600mm horizontally from the edge of the bath or shower tray, or can be situated outside the room if required. Where a ceiling switch is to be used, it must be situated at least 2.25m above floor level, although the cord can be in zone 1 if required.

I prefer to use a wall-mounted switch wherever possible. The reason for this is that there is more space if 10mm² cables are used; these can be difficult to fit into a cord switch mounting box unless a deep box is used. Where the use of a cord switch is

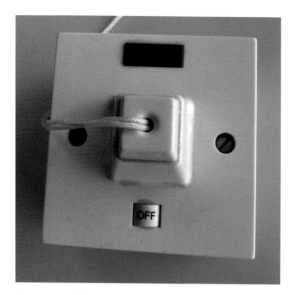

45A cord switch with neon indicator.

unavoidable, it is a good idea to use one that is neon indicated, which will be useful to identify whether or not the shower is on – particularly where the shower itself does not have indicator lamps.

DISTRIBUTION CIRCUITS

A distribution circuit is a circuit that is used to extend an installation. For example, if we were to build an extension onto the back of a house, it may be that the extension required a number of new circuits, because the existing circuits in the original part of the house are fully loaded and new circuits are the only option. To save running many circuits from the extension to the existing consumer unit, it would possibly be more convenient to install a new consumer unit.

The cable that would be run from the origin of the installation to the new consumer unit would be classed as a distribution circuit or a sub-main. The cable would have to be large enough to carry the load required for all of the new circuits. The load could be calculated using diversity, as explained elsewhere in this book. It is always a good idea to allow a larger cable than is required at the time as this will allow for future additions at a later date.

Calculating the Voltage Drop

Let's say we have an extension that has a 6A lighting circuit, which is going to be around 14m in length and is to be wired in $1mm^2$ twin and earth cable. The distribution circuit to the sub-board supplying the circuit is going to be 18m long and all of the circuits in the new distribution board will have a total maximum current of 40A. Before we can calculate the CSA of the distribution circuit, we must first calculate the voltage drop for the worst circuit that is to be connected. This is usually going to be a lighting circuit, as they only have a permitted 3 per cent voltage drop.

Conductor cross sectional area (mm^2)	Voltage drop (mV/A/m)
1	44
1.5	29
2.5	18
4	11
6	7.3
10	4.4

From the table we can see that $1mm^2$ cable has a voltage drop of 44mV/A/m.

The calculation used is:

mV × A × length in metres ÷ 1000 (1000 used to convert to V)

$$\frac{44 \times 6 \times 14}{1000} = 3.69 \text{ volts}$$

The voltage drop for the new lighting circuit will be 3.69V.

This will leave us:

6.9 - 3.69 = 3.21 volts

Permissible voltage drop for the distribution circuit
The simplest method of calculating the size of the cable for this circuit is to use the maximum permissible voltage drop in the calculation:

$$\frac{\text{max permissible} \times 1000}{\text{length} \times \text{total current}} = \text{maximum milli volts}$$

$$\frac{3.21 \times 1000}{18 \times 40} = 4.45 \text{ milli volts}$$

We must now select a cable from the table that has a voltage drop of less than 4.45 mV/A/m. This is going to be a $10mm^2$ cable.

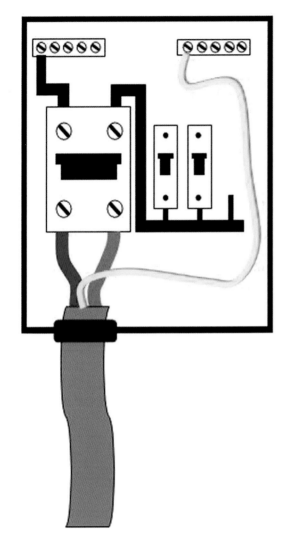

Load end of distribution circuit.

drop for the circuits being connected to it first; this will then give you the figure that must not be exceeded.

Once the cable size has been calculated and the cable installed, it will need to be connected. The end that is connected to the new consumer's unit will need to be connected into the consumer's unit isolator and main earthing terminal.

When terminating the distribution circuit at the origin, there are different options. We can connect into the existing main consumer's unit using a protective device that is suitably rated. This option is fine but it means that if we isolate the board at the origin, the board in the extension will also be isolated. Where the original board is protected by an RCD main switch, the new board would automatically shut down if there was a fault that resulted in the operation of the RCD. This would mean that the new board would also be isolated.

In some instances it may be preferential to terminate the distribution circuit independently of the existing board. This would require the installation of a dedicated isolator, which would need to be connected to the live side of the installation.

The first part of the operation will require the removal of the main supply fuse, as it will be necessary to install a main block into the meter tails between the meter and the existing consumer's unit.

Once the main block is in place, a dedicated device must be installed that will allow protection and isolation of the new distribution circuit.

Another consideration in voltage drop is that we must always remember that the voltage drop permitted is 3 per cent (6.9V) for lighting circuits and 5 per cent (11.5V) for other circuits. This voltage drop is from the origin to the furthest point on the circuit. For this reason the voltage drop on the distribution circuit must be kept as low as possible; this alone often results in the use of a large cable.

The simplest way to decide the voltage drop for the distribution circuit is to calculate the voltage

Mains block.

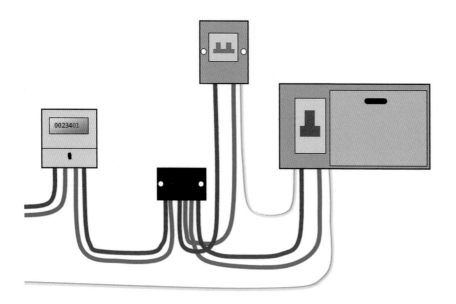

Tails cut into meter tails using a Henley block to provide a supply to a new consumer's unit.

Where the distribution circuit is installed in the building's structure, the cable can either be protected by installing it in an earthed containment system, such as steel conduit, or using a metal sheathed cable, such as a steel-wired armour cable.

Another possibility is to use RCD protection at the supply end of the circuit. This will comply with all of the required regulations, but it will result in all of the circuits in the new board being switched off if there was an earth fault on only one circuit.

The most suitable method in most cases would be to use a steel-wired armoured cable. RCD protection could be provided for each individual circuit on the board supplied from the distribution circuit. In this situation, the distribution circuit must still be provided with overload and short circuit protection.

For this, a one-way consumer's unit could be used and connected by suitably sized meter tails from the main block, along with a suitably sized earthing conductor from the main earthing terminal. Another method would be to install a double pole circuit breaker enclosed in a box with a din rail.

DISTRIBUTION CIRCUIT FOR A REMOTE BUILDING

Where it is required to provide a supply to a remote building, the use of a distribution circuit will be required. The cable size will need to be calculated and a suitable cable route will need to be identified.

By far the best method for most situations will be to bury a steel-wired armour cable, although overhead cables or cables clipped to a wall will also be suitable, if required.

Where the cable is to be buried, there is no regulation that provides a set depth. The rules are that it must be to a suitable depth to prevent damage. In most cases, a depth of 600mm will be sufficient to avoid damage. Of course, where the cable is installed under a concrete drive or path, the depth could be reduced quite considerably. The cable must be laid beneath any hardcore that may be used, as although the SWA is very robust it would become damaged over time if any sharp pieces of hardcore were pressing against it.

In all cases where a cable is buried, certain procedures should be followed. The trench should have a reasonably smooth bottom with no sharp stones

Cable laid in a trench.

protruding. The cable must be installed allowing some slack by snaking it in the trench; this is to allow for any small movement in the ground surrounding the cable.

Once the cable is in the trench, it can be covered by fine soil or sand to a depth of 150mm or so; this is to ensure that there are no sharp stones and the like pressing down on the cable. On top of the fine soil a cable marking tape or tile should be laid, which will indicate to anyone who may be excavating or digging that a cable is present.

The trench can now be filled with the soil that was taken out of it. Always leave the soil a bit high as it will compact over a few weeks. If you leave the soil flush with the ground, you will end up with a bit of a groove, which can be unsightly if it is across a lawn.

When terminating the cable we have some choices in the method that we could use.

Where the supply to the main building is a TT system, it can be extended simply by connecting the supply end to a circuit breaker in the consumer's unit, and terminating the load end into a suitably sized consumer's unit in the remote building, and using the steel-wire armouring of the cable as the circuit protective conductor. The problem with this type of installation is that if a fault were to occur in the remote building, it would trip the RCD in the main building.

One method of overcoming this problem would be to install a separate, small consumer unit in the main building with a 100mA time-delay RCD as a main switch and a suitably rated device for overload and short-circuit protection. The method of connecting a consumer's unit in this way is described in the section for distribution circuits.

A suitably sized consumer's unit could then be installed in the remote building. Depending on the type of installation this could either have a 30mA RCD as a main switch, with circuits protected by circuit breakers, or if preferred, a non-RCD main switch with switch RCBOs for each individual circuit.

When the main supply is a TN-S or a TN-C-S system, my preferred method of installation would be to connect the cable supplying the remote building to a non-RCD protected circuit in the

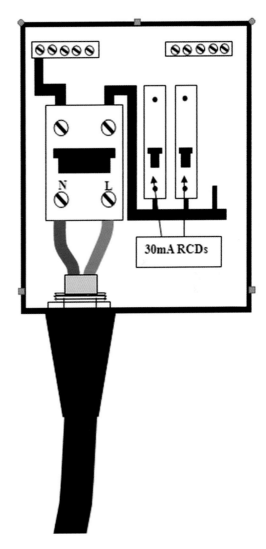

Consumer's unit at remote end of distribution circuit.

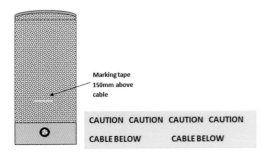

Marking tape
150mm above
cable

CAUTION CAUTION CAUTION CAUTION

CABLE BELOW   CABLE BELOW

Cable with marking tape.

main building. The CPC for this circuit could be the steel-wire armour of the cable, or a separate CPC, depending on the type of cable used.

At the remote building, the cable should be terminated into an insulated box; this will effectively isolate the earth from the building from the remote installation. The live conductors should now be connected into an insulated consumer's unit, which has an RCD main switch or separate RCBOs for each circuit.

An earth electrode should now be installed in a suitable position near the remote building and this should be connected to the consumer's unit in the remote building using a suitably sized earthing conductor; $6mm^2$ will usually be suitable. The remote building will now be a TT system and any faults on the circuits in the remote building will only affect the protective devices in the consumer's unit locally.

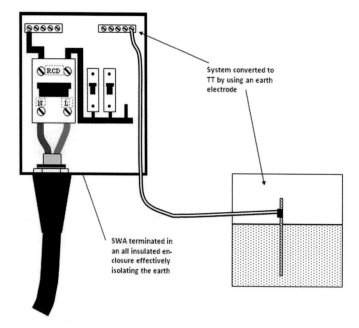

System converted to TT by using an earth electrode

SWA terminated in an all insulated enclosure effectively isolating the earth

Circuit converted to TT system.

CHAPTER 11

Cable Selection

SELECTING THE CORRECT SIZE OF CABLE

Electricians often find cable calculations confusing. For that reason, cables installed are often oversized. When asked why a certain cable has been used, the reply is very often 'because we have always done it that way' or 'because this is how I have been taught'. This approach to circuit design is fine for circuits such as ring circuits serving an area of up to $100m^2$, which are wired in $2.5mm^2$ cable protected by 32A circuit breakers or 30A fuses, and radial socket outlet circuits wired in $4mm^2$ cable protected by 32A circuit breakers or 30A fuses.

However, because it has always been done in a certain way it does not mean that it is the correct way. Every circuit should be designed on its own merits using the tables provided in BS 7671 wiring regulations. It is quite a simple process, provided it is taken a step at a time. All that is required is a little practice.

The first few steps of the process are described as follows.

Calculate the load current, often referred to as the design current. It will be shown as I_b and is the amount of current which the cable will be expected to carry.

$$\frac{\text{power rating of equipment}}{\text{voltage}} = \text{design current}$$

Select a protective device. This will be shown as I_n and the device must have a rating of at least that of the design current.

Decide on the factors which may effect cable temperature; these factors are called rating factors and consist of anything which could affect the cable temperature. These could be:

- Thermal insulation shown as C_i
- The cable grouped with other circuits, shown as C_g
- The ambient temperature of the space in which the cables are to be installed, shown as C_a
- Where a circuit is protected by a rewirable fuse a rating factor of 0.725 is always used and this is shown as C_f

The rating factors can be found in the tables provided. If the factors apply to the cable at the same time, they must all be applied.

For example: a cable is grouped together with a number of circuits (C_g) all passing through thermal insulation (C_i). The ambient temperature around the insulation must also be considered (C_a) and the circuit is protected by a BS 3036 rewirable fuse (C_f). Under these conditions, all factors must be applied.

If, however, the circuits are grouped together for a short run, and then the circuit that we are installing passes through thermal insulation on its own, and then it passes through an area that has an ambient temperature that is likely to increase to above 30°C, only the worst rating factor should be used, along with the rating factor for the rewirable fuse, because they are not having an affect on the cable in the same area. Where a rewirable fuse is used, the C_f of 0.725 must always be used, as it will always have an affect on the cable, and the worst factor will always be the smallest number.

Once the rating factors have been decided on and the values obtained, they must be applied to the current rating of the protective device (I_n):

$$\frac{I_n}{C_g \times C_i \times C_a \times C_f} = I_t$$

I_t is the minimum rating that will be allowed for the cable and can be found in the tables provided.

These are the first few steps for cable selection. If we use them against the following example we will see how it works.

A cable is to be installed for a load of 4.5kW. The circuit is to be wired in twin and earth PVC cable with a maximum temperature rating of 30°C. It will be enclosed in a plastic conduit, which contains one other circuit, and the conduit will be in an insulated wall. The ambient temperature is not going to rise above 30°C and the circuit is going to be protected by a BS 3036 fuse. The circuit is to be connected to a supply system, which is TN-C-S and has a Z_e of 0.35Ω. The length of the cable run is 12m.

Step 1
Calculate I_b:

$$\frac{P}{V} = I$$

$$\frac{4,500}{230} = 19.56A$$

I_b = 19.56A.

Step 2
Select the rating of the protective device.

The nearest BS 3036 fuse equal to or greater than this current rating is 20A

I_n = 20A.

Step 3
Check the table for the correct rating factors C_g.

The conduit contains two circuits, giving a rating factor of 0.8.

The ambient temperature is 30°C and therefore the rating is 1.

Rating factors for ambient temperature (Ca)

Ambient temperature °C	70 °C Thermoplastic Cable
25	1.04
30	1.00
35	0.91
40	0.82
45	0.71

For circuits installed in thermal insulation we have two choices. We can either use a rating factor (C_i), which would require referring to a table for thermal installation, or we can use a much simpler method to compensate for thermal insulation by using an installation reference method for the type of cable being used.

C_f for the rewirable fuse is always 0.725.

Step 4
Divide I_n by the rating factors:

$$\frac{I_n}{C_g \times C_a \times C_f}$$

$$\frac{20}{0.8 \times 1 \times 0.725} = 34.48A$$

The value that has been calculated is the minimum current at which the cable we select is rated. In most calculations this will been seen as:

$$I_t \geq \frac{I_n}{\text{rating factors}}$$

Rating factors for groups of circuits (Cg)

Cable arrangement (Touching cables)	Number of circuits or multicore cables						
	1	2	3	4	5	6	7
Bunched in air, on a surface, chased into a wall or enclosed	1.00	0.80	0.70	0.65	0.60	0.57	0.54
Single layer on the surface of a wall or floor	1.00.	0.85	0.79	0.75	0.73	0.72	0.71
Single layer of multicore on a perforated cable tray	1.00	0.88	0.82	0.77	0.75	0.73	0.73

Current-carrying capacities for flat twin cable

Conductor cross-sectional area 1	Method 100 Above plasterboard ceiling covered by thermal insulation not exceeding 100mm thick 2	Method 101 Above a plasterboard ceiling covered by thermal insulation exceeding 100mm thick 3	Method 102 In a stud wall with thermal insulation with the cable touching the inner wall surface 4	Method 103 In a stud wall with thermal insulation and the cable not touching the inner wall surface 5	Reference method C Clipped direct 6	Reference method A Enclosed in conduit in an insulated wall 7	Voltage drop Per ampere per metre 8
(mm²)	(A)	(A)	(A)	(A)	(A)	(A)	(mV/A/m)
1	13	10.5	13	8	16	11.5	44
1.5	16	13	16	10	20	14.5	29
2.5	21	17	21	13.5	27	20	18
4	27	22	27	17.5	37	26	11
6	34	27	35	23.5	47	32	7.3
10	45	36	47	32	64	44	4.4
16	57	46	63	42.5	85	57	2.8

I_t is the minimum rating for the cable which must now be selected from the current-carrying capacity table for flat twin cables.

Step 5
This is where it gets a little more complicated.

If we look at the table we can see that there are various installation methods.

As our circuit is installed in conduit in a thermally insulated wall, we must use reference method A. This shows that the cable size that can carry 34.48A is a 10mm² cable.

In the example calculation, we used a BS 3036 rewirable fuse. Although the use of rewirable fuses is perfectly acceptable, and in most cases they offer very good protection, the use of them will result in the use of larger cables. In reality, most modern installations use circuit breakers, and where these are used, there is no requirement for us to apply the rating factor C_f as this is only for use with rewirable fuses.

If we carry out the example calculation again without using C_f we can see that it will result in us being able to select a smaller CSA of cable:

$$\frac{20}{0.8 \times 1} = 25A$$

If we now look again at the table, we can see that the cable size has been reduced to 4mm² for the remainder of our example calculation. We will assume that we have changed the protective device from a 20A BS 3036 fuse to a 20A BS EN 60898 type B circuit breaker.

Unfortunately this is not the end of the cable calculation, as we have still to check that the voltage drop is not too high and also that the protective device will operate in the correct time in the event of a fault.

The voltage drop for this circuit must not exceed 5 per cent, which on a supply voltage of 230V is 11.5V. For our single-phase circuits we always use a voltage of 230 for our calculations, even if we measure a higher voltage.

For voltage drop we need to refer once again to the table. Column 8 will show that a 4mm² cable has a voltage drop of 11mV/A for every metre of cable used this is shown as (mV/A/m).

When we are carrying out this calculation we must make sure that we use the actual current that will be in the circuit (I_b), not the rating of the protective device or the cable rating.

Referring back to our example, we can see that the I_b for the circuit is 19.56A and the circuit is 12m long. The calculation is:

$$\frac{mV \times I_b \times length}{1000} = \text{voltage drop}$$

Dividing by 1000 will convert mV to V:

$$\frac{11 \times 19.56 \times 12}{1000} = 2.58 \text{ volts}$$

We can see that the voltage drop for this circuit is 2.58V, which is well within the maximum permitted value.

Next we need to ensure that the protective device will operate within the required time. As this circuit is not greater than 32A, the maximum permitted disconnection time will be 0.4sec.

To calculate the resistance of our circuit we need to refer to the table, which gives us the resistance per metre for our conductors at a temperature of 20°C.

Resistance per metre for conductors at a temperature of 20°C.

Conductor cross-sectional area mm²	Resistance per metre (mΩ/m)
1	18.10
1.5	12.10
2.5	7.41
4.0	4.61
6.0	3.08
10.0	1.83
16.0	1.15

As our cable is 4mm² twin and earth, it will have a 1.5mm² circuit protective conductor (CSA).

From the table we can see that the resistance of a 4mm² conductor is 4.61 mΩ/m; as this is the line conductor it is known as r1.

The resistance of the 1.5mm² conductor is 12.10 mΩ/m and this in known as r2.

We must now add the two values together to give us the resistance of our conductors per metre – this is known as r1 + r2, which for this circuit is 16.71mΩ/m.

As the circuit is 12m long the calculation to find the resistance of this circuit is:

$$\frac{((r)_1 + r_2) \times L}{1000}$$

$$\frac{16.71 \times 12}{1000} = 0.2\Omega$$

We divide by 1000 to convert mΩ to Ω.

0.2Ω is the resistance of our 12m of cable at a temperature of 20°C, and is now $R_1 + R_2$. As we have seen earlier in this book, the temperature of the conductors will rise when we pass a current through the line conductor. When the conductor temperature rises, the conductor's resistance will increase. To compensate for the temperature rise we must multiply $R_1 + R_2$ by a factor of 1.2:

$$0.2 \times 1.2 = 0.24\Omega.$$

This is the value of resistance that we could expect the conductors to have when they are carrying the maximum current.

Now we need to add the external resistance Z_e to the calculated $R_1 + R_2$ and this will give us the maximum value of resistance (impedance) for the circuit (Z_s). This is the resistance from the furthest point of a circuit right back to the supply transformer through the line and earth of both the final circuit cable and the supply cable.

From our example $Z_e = 0.35\Omega$.

$$Z_s = Z_e + R_1 + R_2$$

$$0.35 + 0.24 = 0.59\Omega.$$

Our actual value of Z_s is 0.59Ω.

This must now be compared to the maximum Z_s permissible for the protective device being used, which can be found in the tables.

Type B circuit breakers and the overcurrent characteristics of RCBOs to BS EN 61009-1

Rating Amps	3	6	10	16	20	25	32	40	50
Z_s Ω		11.65	5.87	3.5	2.3	1.75	1.4	1.1	0.88	0.7

Type C circuit breakers and the overcurrent characteristics of RCBOs to BS EN 61009-1

Rating Amps	3	6	10	16	20	25	32	40	50
Z_s Ω		5.82	2.91	1.75	1.09	0.87	0.7	0.55	0.44	0.35

The Z_s values for D type breakers have not been provided as they are not suitable for use in most domestic situations.

This shows us that the maximum permissible Z_s

for the circuit would be 1.75Ω. As the total Z_s for the circuit is 0.59Ω, which is less than the maximum permitted, this circuit will be suitable.

Having carried out the calculation we can now wire the circuit in $4mm^2$ live conductors with a $1.5mm^2$.

This looks quite a long calculation but this is because I have explained each step in detail. The process in simplified form is as follows:

- Calculate I_b.
- Select a protective device I_n, which must be greater or equal to I_b.
- Identify the rating factors C_a, C_g, C_i or C_f.
- Divide I_n by the relevant rating factors to give a value for I_t.
- Identify the correct installation reference method.
- Select a cable size from the correct table for the type of cable being used.
- Check voltage drop.
- Calculate $R_1 + R_2$ and add to Z_e to find the actual circuit Z_s.
- Look up the maximum permitted Z_s for the protective device and compare it with the actual circuit Z_s.
- Providing the actual circuit Z_s is less than the maximum permitted, the cable selected will be suitable.

SURGE PROTECTION

Over the years the electrical equipment which we use has become very complex, with most items of equipment making use of electronic components. These components can be very sensitive, particularly to overvoltages. Even small overvoltages which are in the system for micro seconds can significantly reduce the lifespan of equipment.

These overvoltages can be caused by direct lighting strikes or more often indirect lighting strikes, perhaps to a nearby tall structure or tree. They can also be caused by switching of heavy loads particularly inductive loads.

The wiring regulations require that surge protection is provided for all installations other than dwellings where the total value of the installation and equipment being protected does not justify the cost of the protection.

In reality the cost of a type 2 surge protection device would add less than a £100 to the cost of a rewire, or consumers unit change. They simply take up 1 or sometimes 2 spaces on a din rail.

There are 3 types of surge protection devices, type 1 would be installed where a property has lightning protection, or where it is near a tall building or where it is on a hilltop in a lightning prone area.

A type 1 protection device is used to protect the hard wiring of an electrical installation and would be installed at the origin of the installation. This type of device would not normally be installed in a domestic installation unless it was high risk as described previously.

Type 2 surge protection devices would normally be installed in consumers units or distribution boards, these are used to prevent overvoltages spreading within the installation and protects equipment connected to it.

Type 3 surge protective devices would not normally be used alone but be used as added protection to supplement type 2 devices, particularly in areas which contain items of sensitive equipment.

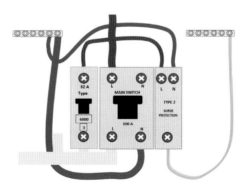

ABOVE: *Domestic surge protection.*
RIGHT: *Typical connection method.*

CHAPTER 12

Photovoltaic Microgeneration Systems

The installation of solar photovoltaic systems can be a very good way to reduce a household's fuel bill, particularly as the cost of electricity is likely to keep rising.

It has been calculated that for each square metre of surface area directly facing the sun, approximately 1000W of energy could be captured. Photovoltaic panels can be used to capture this energy and turn it into electricity, which can then be used or sold to your distribution network operator (DNO).

Although the cost of the equipment is quite high, once installed all of the energy produced will be free and a feed-in tariff will be paid to the owner of the system. At the moment the tariff is guaranteed for twenty-five years, which means that the cost of the installed equipment will be repaid over a period of time.

Unfortunately, although it is possible to install this equipment yourself, the feed-in tariff can only be claimed for installations that have been installed by a registered microgeneration scheme (MCS) inspector.

Providing the installation does not exceed 16A per phase, permission will not be required from the DNO.

Before any installation, it is vitally important that a survey is carried out on the property to ensure that it is suitable. Providing the building is not listed or in a conservation area, planning permission will not normally be required, as the installation would be classed as permitted development. It is always a good idea to check with the local planning authority before commencing any work on the outside of a building.

Where planning is not required, it is still a requirement to comply with the planning regulations. The one that would affect most installations is that the panels must not protrude more than 200mm above the roof, and must not be higher than the ridge of the roof.

In some situations it may be more suitable to install the panels on a flat roof, or even in the garden. There are also rules for these installations and a trip or a phone call to the planning office may save you some problems. It would be an expensive mistake to install a PV system only to find that you have to take it out again.

For the installation of PV to be a viable proposition, the roof on which it is to be installed must face between east and west; the nearer to south that the solar panels face, the better the performance of the system will be.

Once it has been ascertained that the roof is facing in a suitable direction, a check must be carried out to see if any shadows are likely to be cast over the panels at any time during the day. Where shadows are likely, the panels must be installed to avoid them. Any shading at all will have a huge effect on the output of the system, and in some cases the system will become damaged.

The roof must now be checked for structural suitability and the condition of the tiles. It would be very dangerous to install a system on a roof that was not strong enough to withstand the additional load and not very sensible if the condition of the tiles or slates was poor. A structural survey should be carried out on the roof before installation.

It is usually a good idea to seek the advice of a structural engineer, particularly when the installation is to be installed onto an older property.

The next part of the exercise is to calculate how many panels can be fitted onto the roof. The easiest method is to measure the size of the roof and then get the supplier of the panels to work it out for you.

If you choose to do it yourself, you must first measure the roof and then find out from the supplier what the size of each panel will be. Once you have this information it is a simple process to draw to scale the roof with the panels on. Never allow the panels to fit flush with the eaves, this will prevent problems due to wind lift. As a general rule, the panels should be 10 per cent of the width of the roof from the eaves and 10 per cent of the depth from the verge.

Once you have decided how many panels could be fixed to the roof, it will be possible to calculate how much energy that it will be possible for the installation to generate.

Before calculating the installation output you will need some information about the panels. Each type of panel will have been tested under what is known as standard test conditions (STC). This is to ensure that when you purchase a panel, you can be provided with information about it that can be used to compare with other makes of panels.

Each manufacturer must have their panels tested at a temperature of 25°C against an irradiance of 1000W. The air mass must also be carefully controlled and the test is carried out at an air mass of 1.5; the current generated will be d.c.

The test will provide the open circuit voltage (Voc) and the short circuit current (Isc) for the panel. Depending on the type and quality of panel, these values will vary. Remember, PV panels are not very efficient. As we have seen, one square metre of area directly facing the sun will produce 1kW of energy. Unfortunately PV panels are usually less then 20 per cent efficient.

For our example calculation, we can use the values from a typical panel which I fitted recently:

Voc = 44.2V
Isc = 5.1A
Peak power output (Pmax) = 180W

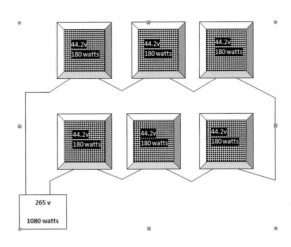

Six PV panels as a string.

The panels can be connected in series to form a string. The number of panels in a string will depend on the voltage that is required.

Let's consider a roof where it is possible to install twelve photovoltaic panels.

If we connect six of the panels in series, we increase the voltage and will have a final voltage of:

$$6 \times 44.2 = 265.2V \text{ (Voc)}$$

and an output of:

$$6 \times 180 = 1080W.$$

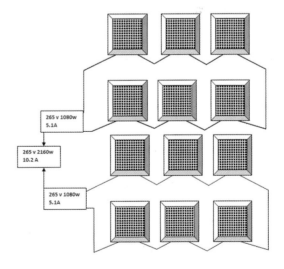

Two strings of six panels in parallel.

The current will not increase when panels are connected in series.

As we have twelve panels, we can have two strings, which can be connected in parallel. When panels are connected in parallel, the voltage remains the same but the current will increase.

The installation will now have an output of 265.2V (Voc). With a Pmax of:

$$12 \times 180 = 2160W$$

and a current (Isc) of:

$$2 \times 5.1 = 10.2A.$$

As the current supplied by the PV system will be direct current, it will need to be converted into alternating current. This will require the use of a piece of equipment that is called an inverter.

The inverter must be matched to the output of the photovoltaic array. It is important that the correct inverter is used, as its purpose is not only to convert d.c current to a.c current, it will also allow any excess energy to be transported back into the National Grid at the correct frequency.

Once you have decided on the size of the system and the type of panels that are going to be used, access to the roof is the next consideration. The installation of solar panels is not a job that can be carried out from ladders. Although the panels are usually around 20kg, they are very awkward

Selection of roof hooks.

Inverter.

to carry and can be easily damaged. Fixed scaffolding, which has been erected by a professional scaffolding contractor, is by far the best method. The correct access will not only make the job easier, it will also make it much safer. Of course other methods can be used and each installation will have to have its access considered, depending on site conditions.

Fixing the panels to the roof is not a difficult job, providing the correct equipment is used. Roof hooks must first be fixed to the roof rafters and they must be suitable for the type of tile or slate that has been used for the roof covering.

There are many types of roof hooks available to suit all types of roofing.

The roof hooks must be securely fixed to the rafters and not the tile battens. Once they have been fixed, the slates/tiles must be carefully replaced; in some cases a lead flashing may be required.

Once the roof hooks are in place, there are various methods for fixing the mounting rails to the hooks.

Roof hooks fitted and slates replaced.

The panels can now be fixed to the rails using the appropriate clips. As the panels are fixed, they must be connected together. Each panel will have two wires connected to it: one will be positive (+) and the other negative (−). As the panels are fixed, the positive of one panel will be fixed to the negative of the panel next to it. On completion of the fixing of one string, there will be one positive and one negative connector, which must be passed through the tiles into the roof space. It will probably be easier to pass new cables through the roof and then fix connectors to the ends ready to connect to the panels.

Before the panels are carried up onto the roof, it is essential that they are inspected for damage and tested for correct operation. The test is quite simple and at this stage is only a matter of using a multimeter to carry out a voltage test on each panel. For the panels that are used in the example, the multimeter must be set on d.c. voltage to the nearest value above 44.2V. A short-circuit test can also be carried out by joining the panel connectors together and using a clamp meter to measure the current.

Great care must be taken where the cables pass from outside the roof to inside. The cables must be free to move as there will be expansion and contraction on the roof due to climate changes throughout the year. A good method of passing the cables through the roof is to use a roof vent tile or a purpose-made lead slate with cable glands attached to it. Although the cables are very robust, they must never be allowed just to enter the roof between tiles without some type of protection.

LEFT AND ABOVE: *Mounting rails.*

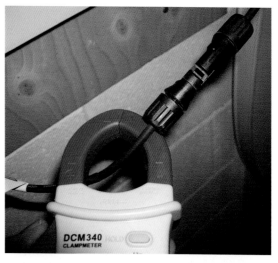

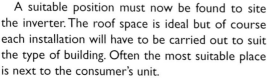

ABOVE: *Voltage check on panels.*
RIGHT: *Short-circuit current test.*

A suitable position must now be found to site the inverter. The roof space is ideal but of course each installation will have to be carried out to suit the type of building. Often the most suitable place is next to the consumer's unit.

It is possible to site the inverter anywhere that is suitable and compliant with manufacturers' instructions. Ventilation is very important because, when the inverter is working, it will produce heat that must be allowed to dissipate. There must also be enough space to fit the required isolators.

Wherever it is decided to place the inverter, the cables must be run to it from where they enter the roof. There are various methods and types of cables that can be used; however, cable that has been manufactured purposely for the job is the best option as it meets all of the requirements.

Where these cables are to be run through the roof space, they can be clipped directly to the surface providing they are clearly identified using labels. It is

Cable passing into roof space.

also a good idea to identify the positive and negative cable by wrapping brown tape around the positive and grey around the negative at suitable intervals.

Where the installation uses two strings in parallel, the cables from each string can be joined in the roof as near to where they enter the roof as possible. This will save having to run two sets of cables to the inverter, which of course will make the installation easier and slightly less expensive.

The connection of multiple strings can be made by using a junction box. The preferred way of joining d.c. cables is by using crimp connectors. In all cases the junction box must be clearly labelled to indicate that the connections inside the box will be live during daylight.

Another method of connecting multiple strings is to use a connector made specifically for the job.

Although the PV panels will have connectors pre-fitted to the cable ends, it will be necessary

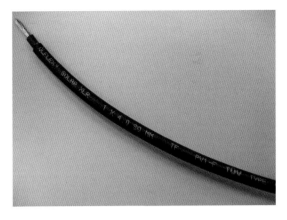

Solar cable.

to fit connectors to the ends of any cables used to run between the panels and the inverter. These connectors must be purpose-made and will be either type three or four connectors. Unfortunately,

Correct label for PV junction box.

PV Array
Junction Box
DANGER
Contains live parts
during daylight

BELOW: Solar PV connectors.

Male PV connector.

Female PV connector.

manufacturers do not make them all to the same specification. Often the connectors fitted to the panels will not be compatible with the connectors that you need to use to extend the cables. In these situations it is simple just to cut the connectors off from the panel and replace them with the same type that you are going to use.

The connectors must, of course, be connected to the correct ends: the positive connector is the male. The negative connector will be the female. Both are clearly identified with (+) positive and (−) negative.

It is reasonably easy to terminate the cables to the connector. Some connectors require the use of a crimp, although my preferred connector is the type that fix to the cable using a pressure spring.

When the d.c. cables have been installed, they must be terminated into a d.c. switch disconnector, which is rated to the requirements of the installation. The use of a d.c. switch for this is very

important, as direct current will create a large arc between the switch contacts when the installation is turned off. This switch must be clearly labelled. For installations consisting of three strings or fewer, there is no need for any protection, such as fuses or circuit breakers, to be provided on the d.c. side of the installation.

For practical and safety reasons it is always better to install and connect the d.c. isolator before connecting the panels to the system. Once the panels are connected, the system will be live up to the d.c. isolator. By installing and connecting the isolator first, it will not be necessary to work with live d.c. cables.

Once the d.c. isolator has been installed and connected, the rest of the installation can be connected. The d.c. switch must be connected to the inverter using the correct terminations which will usually be provided with the inverter.

From the outgoing side of the inverter, the system will be a.c. and all of the installation will have to comply with the BS 7671 wiring regulations.

From the consumer's unit a cable of the correct rating must be connected to the outgoing side of a protective device; this device must be dedicated to the PV system only.

An a.c. isolator must be provided near to the consumer's unit, to provide isolation for the inverter.

Solar PV crimp connector.

Spring connector.

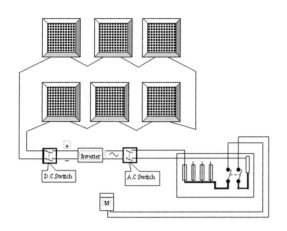

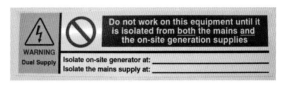

ABOVE: Dual isolation notice.

LEFT: Solar PV system.

Where the inverter is installed away from the consumer's unit, two isolators will be required. One will be next to the consumer's unit and the other next to the inverter; both must have notices attached indicating there are two or more points of isolation.

Between the isolator and the inverter a generation meter must be installed. The generation meter is used to record all of the energy that is generated by the PV installation and will be used to calculate the amount of money due to be paid by the DNO.

On completion of the installation, a range of inspections and tests must be carried out before it is energized. It is also a requirement that certification is completed, some of it required by the DNO before they will agree to pay the feed-in tariff.

The certification and inspecting and testing are explained in detail in Chapter 13.

Where the PV array is to be installed as a freestanding installation in a garden or on a flat roof, the electrical requirements are the same, although for obvious reasons the method of fixing the panels will be different.

For a flat-roof installation it is possible to use frames that are made at an angle of 35 degrees. All that is required is for the frame to be secured with the panel facing as near to south as possible. Where fixing through a flat roof may present a problem, mounting boxes may be used. These are held in place by putting bags of sand or some other weighty substance in the box and then fixing the panel to the box.

ABOVE: Flat roof frame.

RIGHT: PV mounting box.

CHAPTER 13

Inspection, Testing and Certification

Whenever we install a new circuit or carry out alterations or additions to an electrical installation, it is a requirement that we complete a certificate to show that the work has been inspected and tested for compliance with the current edition of the wiring regulations BS 7671.

In a domestic installation this requirement is part of the building regulation part P. As I have explained earlier in this book, failure to comply with building regulations is a very serious offence. At times this can be enforced with heavy fines and, even on occasion, imprisonment.

Clearly installing circuits and completing all of the other work that goes along with it carefully is very important, but in many ways the final step, which is the initial verification of a new circuit, could be seen as being the most important part of the job.

We all make mistakes occasionally, and sometimes materials and equipment will be found to be defective. The initial verification of circuits will, if carried out correctly, identify these mistakes or defects. If we have carried out a rewire of an installation, or wired a new installation, the inspection and test will involve more than one circuit. However, although we can look at an installation as a whole, we still have to test each circuit individually.

For a new circuit or a new installation we will need to complete an electrical installation certificate. This should also include a schedule of test results and a schedule of inspections. An alteration that results in a change of protective device or the installation of an RCD will also require the completion of this certificate.

A single electrical installation certificate can be used for a complete installation, the addition of a single circuit or an alteration. Once a certificate has been completed, it cannot be added to at a later date, and if other work is carried out on the installation, a new certificate must be produced, regardless of whether it is for a complete new circuit or simply installing a different protective device.

INITIAL VERIFICATION

A visual inspection must be carried out before any testing. One reason for this is to ensure that the installation or circuit is safe to test.

BS 7671 indicates that we must carry out an inspection to ensure that:

- All equipment complies with a British or acceptable European standard.
- Every part of the installation undergoing initial verification has been selected and erected in accordance with BS 7671 and complies with the manufacturers' instructions.
- The new installation is not visibly damaged or has any defects which may impair safety.

Whenever we carry out an initial verification we must complete an electrical installation certificate. This certificate can only be issued for work that meets the standards set out in BS 7671. Where a non-compliance is present on the part of the installation being certified, it must be put right before the certificate is issued.

The certificates are shown in BS 7671 as three separate documents: the electrical installation certificate, a schedule of inspections and a schedule of test results. Some electrical registration bodies have an electrical installation certificate, which includes all three on a single document.

COMPLETING AN ELECTRICAL INSTALLATION CERTIFICATE

The electrical installation certificate must include the address and description of the installation, and whether it is domestic, commercial or some other type of installation.

It must also provide clear information on:

- What work has been carried out (extent of the installation).
- Is it a new installation? This would include a complete new installation or a rewire.
- Is it an addition to an installation? This could be a single or more circuits added to an existing installation.
- Is it an alteration to an existing installation? This may be the change of a consumer's unit or the installation of an RCD to an existing circuit.
- Who has designed, installed and inspected it? This could be the same person.
- What type of supply is it? TT, TN-S, TN-C-S?
- Is it single-phase or three-phase?

Information on the supply will need to be recorded:

- The nominal voltage – U is the voltage between phases and U_0 is the voltage between one phase and earth. If the supply is single-phase, then U_0 will usually be 230V, if three-phase, then 230/400V will need to be entered.
- Frequency – this will be 50Hz.
- Prospective fault current I_{pf}, which is the maximum value of current that could flow in an electrical installation.
- External earth loop impedance Z_e, which is the value of resistance of the line and earth measured from the origin of the supply to the supply transformer. It can be obtained by enquiry if measurement is not possible.

- Type and rating of supply fuse, which is normally marked on the side of the fuse.

Particulars of the installation to which the certificate refers to:

- Type of earthing – is the system earthed using the supplier's facility or has an earth electrode been used?
- Maximum demand in kVA or A – this will be the value after taking into account diversity.
- If an earth electrode has been installed, what type is it? Where is it? What is the electrode resistance?
- Size and material of earthing conductor.
- Size and material of main protective bonding conductors.
- What services have been bonded – gas, oil, water?
- Type of main switch, number of poles, voltage and current rating.
- RCD operating current in mA ($I_{\Delta n}$) and the operating time in ms at($I_{\Delta n}$).
- Where the installation certificate is for an alteration or an addition, comments on the existing installation should be recorded.
- A record of the number of schedules of inspection and schedules of test results that have been completed, along with the electrical installation certificate, must be entered. This will only be more than one schedule of inspection or one schedule of test results, if the installation has more than one consumer unit.

COMPLETING A SCHEDULE OF INSPECTIONS

Before any testing is carried out it is necessary to inspect the installation. One of the main reasons for this is to ensure that the installation is complete and it is safe to carry out the required tests.

When completing a schedule of inspections, the same document needs to be completed for a complete installation or a single circuit. The difference is that if it is for a complete installation, each circuit has to be considered. For a single circuit, only the items that affect the circuit being inspected need to be checked.

Megger.

Certificate No: 2

ELECTRICAL INSTALLATION CERTIFICATE

(REQUIREMENTS FOR ELECTRICAL INSTALLATIONS BS7671 [IET WIRING REGULATIONS])

DETAILS OF THE CLIENT
Client:
Address:

INSTALLATION ADDRESS
Occupier:
Address:

DESCRIPTION AND EXTENT OF THE INSTALLATION
Description of Installation

New installation ☐

Addition to an existing installation ☐

Alteration to an existing installation ☐

Extent of installation covered by this Certificate:

(use continuation sheet if necessary)   see continuation sheet No:

FOR DESIGN, CONSTRUCTION, INSPECTION AND TESTING
I being the person responsible for the Design, Construction, Inspection & Testing of the electrical installation (as indicated by my signature below), particulars of which are described above, having exercised reasonable skill and care when carrying out that Design, Construction, Inspection & Testing, hereby CERTIFY that the design work for which I have been responsible is to the best of my knowledge and belief in accordance with BS7671: 2018 amended to   except for any departures, if any, detailed as follows.
Details of departures from BS7671 (Regulations 120.3 and 133.5):

Details of permitted exceptions (Regulation 411.3.3). Where applicable, a suitable risk assessment(s) must be attached to this certificate.

Risk assessment attached ☐

The extent of liability of the signatory is limited to the work described above as the subject of this Certificate.
Name (IN BLOCK LETTERS)   Date:
Company: Chris Kitcher
Address: 14 Ockenden Way
Signature:

Tel No:
Hassocks

NEXT INSPECTION
I the designer, recommend that this installation is further inspected and tested after an interval of not more than

Page 1 of 6

This form was developed by Megger Limited and is based on the model shown in Appendix 6 of BS7671 : 2018   © Megger Limited 2018

Electrical installation certificate (continued opposite).

SUPPLY CHARACTERISTICS AND EARTHING ARRANGEMENTS

Earthing arrangements

TN-C ☐
TN-S ☐
TN-C-S ☐
TT ☐
IT ☐

Other source of supply (as detailed on attached schedule)

Number and Type of Live Conductors

AC ☐
1-Phase,2-Wire ☐
2-Phase,3-Wire ☐
3-Phase,3-Wire ☐
3-Phase,4-Wire ☐

DC ☐
2-wire ☐
3-wire ☐
Other ☐

Confirmation of supply polarity ☐

Nature of Supply Parameters

Nominal voltage, U/U_0 [(1)]   V

Nominal frequency, f [(1)]   Hz

Prospective fault current, I_{pf} [(2)]   kA

External loop impedance, Z_e [(2)]   Ω

(Note: (1) by enquiry, (2) by enquiry or by measurement)

Supply Protective Device Characteristics

BS (EN)

Type

Rated Current   A

PARTICULARS OF INSTALLATION REFERRED TO IN THE CERTIFICATE

Means of Earthing

Distributor's Facility ☐

Installation Earth Electrode ☐

Maximum Demand

Maximum demand (load)

Details of installation Earth Electrode: *(where applicable)*

Type: *(e.g. rod(s), tape etc)*   Location: Electrode resistance to earth:

    Ω

Main Protective Conductors

| Earthing Conductor | Material | csa | mm 2 | Connection / continuity verified | ☐ |
| Main protective bonding conductors (to extraneous-conductive-parts) | Material | csa | mm 2 | Connection / continuity verified | ☐ |

| To water installation pipes ☐ | To gas installation pipes ☐ | To oil installation pipes ☐ | To structural steel ☐ |

| To lightning protection ☐ | To other ☐ | Specify |

Main Switch / Switch-Fuse / Circuit-Breaker / RCD

Location:

BS, Type:

No of poles:

Current rating: A

Fuse / device rating or setting: A

Voltage rating: V

If RCD main switch

Rated residual operating current $I_{\Delta n}$ mA

Rated time delay   ms

Measured operating time   ms

COMMENTS ON EXISTING INSTALLATION
(in the case of an alteration or additions see Regulation 644.1.2):

SCHEDULES

The attached schedules are part of this document and this Certificate is valid only when they are attached to it.

Schedules of Inspections and   Schedules of Test Results are attached.

(Enter quantities of schedules attached)

Electrical installation certificate (continued).

Certificate No: **2**

SCHEDULE OF INSPECTIONS (for new installation work only) for
DOMESTIC AND SIMILAR PREMISES WITH UP TO 100 A SUPPLY

NOTE 1: This form is suitable for many types of smaller installation not exclusively domestic.

All items inspected in order to confirm, as appropriate, compliance with the relevent clauses in BS7671.
The list of items and associated examples where given are not exhaustive.

NOTE 2: Insert ✓ to indicate an inspection has been carried out and the result is satisfactory, or N/A to indicate that
the inspection is not applicable to a particular item.

ITEM NO	DESCRIPTION	OUTCOME See Note 2
1.0	**EXTERNAL CONDITION OF INTAKE EQUIPMENT (VISUAL INSPECTION ONLY)**	
1.1	Service cable	
1.2	Service head	
1.3	Earthing arrangement	
1.4	Meter tails	
1.5	Metering equipment	
1.6	Isolator (where present)	
2.0	**PARALLEL OR SWITCHED ALTERNATIVE SOURCES OF SUPPLY**	
2.1	Adequate arrangements where a generating set operates as a switched alternative to the public supply (551.6)	
2.2	Adequate arrangements where a generating set operates in parallel with the public supply (551.7)	
3.0	**AUTOMATIC DISCONNECTION OF SUPPLY**	
3.1	**Presence and adequacy of earthing and protective bonding arrangements:**	
	• Distributor's earthing arrangement (542.1.2.1; 542.1.2.2)	
	• Installation earth electrode (where applicable) (542.1.2.3)	
	• Earthing conductor and connections, including accessibility (542.3; 543.3.2)	
	• Main protective bonding conductors and connections including accessibility (411.3.1.2; 543.3.2; 544.1)	
	• Provision of safety electrical earthing / bonding labels at all appropriate locations (514.13)	
	• RCD(s) provided for fault protection (411.4.204; 411.5.3)	
4.0	**BASIC PROTECTION**	
4.1	**Presence and adequacy of measures to provide basic protection (prevention of contact with live parts) within the installation:**	
	• Insulation of live parts e.g. conductors completely covered with durable insulating materials (416.1)	
	• Barriers or enclosures e.g. correct IP rating (416.2)	
5.0	**ADDITIONAL PROTECTION**	
5.1	**Presence and effectiveness of additional protection methods:**	
	• RCD(s) not exceeding 30 mA operating current (415.1; Part 7), see item 8.14 of this schedule	
	• Supplementary bonding (415.2; Part 7)	
6.0	**OTHER METHODS OF PROTECTION**	
6.1	**Presence and effectiveness of methods which give both basic and fault protection:**	
	• SELV systems, including the source and associated circuits (414)	
	• PELV systems, including the source and associated circuits (414)	
	• Double or reinforced insulation i.e. Class II or equivalent equipment and associated circuits (412)	
	• Electrical separation for one item of equipment e.g. shaver supply unit (413)	
7.0	**CONSUMER UNIT(S) / DISTRIBUTION BOARD(S):**	
7.1	Adequacy of access and working space for items of electrical equipment including switchgear (132.12)	
7.2	Components are suitable according to assembly manufacturer's instructions or literature (536.4.203)	
7.3	Presence of linked main switch(es) (462.1.201)	
7.4	Isolators, for every circuit or group of circuits and all items of equipment (462.2)	
7.5	Suitability of enclosure(s) for IP and fire ratings (416.2; 421.1.6; 421.1.201; 526.5)	
7.6	Protection against mechanical damage where cables enter equipment (522.8.1; 522.8.5; 522.8.11)	
7.7	Confirmation that ALL conductor connections are correctly located in terminals and are tight and secure (526.1)	

Page 3 of 6

This form was developed by Megger Limited and is based on the model shown
in Appendix 6 of BS7671: 2018   © Megger Limited 2018

Schedule of Inspections (continued opposite).

Certificate No: 2

ITEM NO	DESCRIPTION	OUTCOME See Note 2
7.0	**CONSUMER UNIT(S) / DISTRIBUTION BOARD (S) continued**	
7.8	Avoidance of heating effects where cables enter ferromagnetic enclosures e.g. steel (521.5)	
7.9	Selection of correct type and ratings of circuit protective devices for overcurrent and fault protection (411.3.2; 411.4, 411.5, 411.6; 432, 433; 537.3.1.1)	
7.10	**Presence of appropriate circuit charts, warning and other notices:**	
	• Provision of circuit charts/schedules or equivalent forms of information (514.9)	
	• Warning notice of method of isolation where live parts not capable of being isolated by a single device (514.11)	
	• Periodic inspection and testing notice (514.12.1)	
	• RCD six-monthly test notice; where required (514.12.2)	
	• AFDD six-monthly test notice; where required	
	• Warning notice of non-standard (mixed) colours of conductors present (514.14)	
7.11	Presence of labels to indicate the purpose of switchgear and protective devices (514.1.1; 514.8)	
8.0	**CIRCUITS**	
8.1	Adequacy of conductors for current-carrying capacity with regard to type and nature of the installation (523)	
8.2	Cable installation methods suitable for the location(s) and external influences (522)	
8.3	Segregation/separation of Band I (ELV) and Band II (LV) circuits, and electrical and non-electrical services (528)	
8.4	Cables correctly erected and supported throughout including escape routes, with protection against abrasion (521, 522)	
8.5	Provision of fire barriers, sealing arrangements where necessary (527.2)	
8.6	Non-sheathed cables enclosed throughout in conduit, ducting or trunking (521.10.1; 526.8)	
8.7	Cables concealed under floors, above ceilings or in walls / partitions, adequately protected against damage (522.6.201; 522.6.202, 522.6.203, 522.6.204)	
8.8	Conductors correctly identified by colour, lettering or numbering (514)	
8.9	Presence, adequacy and correct termination of protective conductors (411.3.1.1; 543.1)	
8.10	Cables and conductors correctly connected, enclosed and with no undue mechanical strain (526)	
8.11	No basic insulation of a conductor visible outside enclosure (526.8)	
8.12	Single-pole devices for switching or protection in line conductors only (132.14.1; 530.3.3; 643.6)	
8.13	Accessories not damaged, securely fixed, correctly connected, suitable for external influences (134.1.1;512.2; Section 526)	
8.14	**Provision of additional protection by RCD not exceeding 30mA:**	
	• Socket-outlets rated at 32 A or less, unless exempt (411.3.3)	
	• Supplies for Mobile equipment with a current rating not exceeding 32 A for use outdoors (411.3.3)	
	• Cables concealed in walls at a depth of less than 50 mm (522.6.202; 522.6.203)	
	• Cables concealed in walls / partitions containing metal parts regardless of depth (522.6.202; 522.6.203)	
	• Final circuits supplying luminaires within domestic (household) premises (411.3.4)	
8.15	**Presence of appropriate devices for isolation and switching correctly located including:**	
	• Means of switching off for mechanical maintenance (Section 464; 537.3.2)	
	• Emergency switching (465.1; 537.3.3)	
	• Functional switching, for control of parts of the installation and current-using equipment (463.1; 537.3.1)	
	• Firefighter's switches (537.4)	
9.0	**CURRENT-USING EQUIPMENT (PERMANENTLY CONNECTED)**	
9.1	Equipment not damaged, securely fixed and suitable for external influences (134.1.1; 416.2; 512.2)	
9.2	Provision of overload and/or undervoltage protection e.g. for rotating machines, if required (Sections 445; 552)	
9.3	Installed to minimize the build-up of heat and restrict the spread of fire (421.1.4; 559.4.1)	
9.4	Adequacy of working space. Accessibility to equipment (132.12; 513.1)	
10.0	**LOCATION(S) CONTAINING A BATH OR SHOWER (SECTION 701)**	
10.1	30 mA RCD protection for all LV circuits, equipment suitable for the zones, supplementary bonding (where required) etc.	
11.0	**OTHER PART 7 SPECIAL INSTALLATIONS OR LOCATIONS**	
11.1	List all other special installations or locations present, if any. (Record separately the results of particular inspections applied)	

Inspected by:

Name (Capitals)   Signature   Date

This form was developed by Megger Limited and is based on the model shown in Appendix 6 of BS7671: 2018 © Megger Limited 2018

Schedule of Inspections (continued).

GENERIC SCHEDULE OF TEST RESULTS

Certificate No: 1

DB reference no
Location
Zs at DB Ω
Ipf at DB (kA)
Correct supply polarity confirmed
Phase sequence confirmed (where appropriate)

Details of circuits and/or installed equipment vulnerable to damage when testing

Details of test instruments used (state serial and/or asset numbers)
Continuity
Insulation resistance
Earth fault loop impedance
RCD
Earth electrode resistance

Tested by:
Name (Capitals)
Signature
Date

Circuit number	Circuit Description	Circuit Details						Protective device				Conductor details			Ring final circuit continuity Ω			Continuity Ω (R1 + R2) or R2		Insulation Resistance Test Voltage	Insulation Resistance (MΩ)		Polarity	Zs Ω	RCD		AFDD	Remarks (continue on a seperate sheet if necessary)
		BS (EN)	type	rating (A)	breaking capacity (kA)	RCD IΔn (mA)	Maximum permitted zs (Ω*)	Reference Method	Live (mm2)	cpc (mm2)	r1 (line)	rn (neutral)	r2 (cpc)	(R1 + R2)	R2	V	Live - Live	Live - Earth		Maximum measured	Disconnection time (ms)	RCD test button operation	Manual AFDD test button operation	
1	2	3	4	5	6	7	8	9	10	11	12	13	14	15	16	17	18	19	20	21	22	23	24	25

Test results

* Where the maximum permitted earth fault loop impedance value stated in column 8 is taken from a source other than the tabulated values given in Chapter 41 of this Standard, state the source of the data in the appropriate cell for the circuit in the 'Remarks' column (column 25) of the schedule.

Schedule of test results.

As an example, for a complete house rewire it is highly likely that the inspection will include a shaver socket; this will come under the heading of electrical separation and the box will need to be ticked. If the same house were to have a single circuit, such as a radial circuit for a socket outlet, that particular circuit will have nothing to do with the shaver socket and for that reason N/A should be entered into the box.

SCHEDULE OF TEST RESULTS

A schedule of test results is a document onto which all of the details of each circuit must be recorded. This requires some information that can be gathered during the inspection and before any testing is started.

The first items to be entered onto the schedule are to provide general information about the installation and who has been responsible for carrying it out.

We need to record which type of supply the system is connected to – is it TT/TN-S or TN-C-S? Each circuit needs a description, the type and rating of the protective device and the size of the conductors.

The method of fault protection for the circuit needs to be recorded. For most circuits this will be 'automatic disconnection of supply', which we can enter as ADS.

Once we have this information, we can begin testing. Each circuit must be subjected to a range of tests and, as this is an initial verification, it should not be carried out on a percentage basis.

The tests carried for an initial verification must be carried out in the correct sequence for safety reasons and to avoid having to repeat tests due to a test failing, which may have had an affect on a previous test.

The sequence of tests is as follows, and it is important that the dead tests are carried out before the installation is connected to the supply.

Dead tests:

- Continuity of protective conductors, which includes main and supplementary bonding conductors.

- Continuity of ring final circuits.
- Insulation resistance.
- Polarity.

Live tests:

- Earth loop impedance Z_e and Z_s.
- Prospective fault current.
- Functional testing, which includes the testing of RCDs for correct operation.

As we carry out the testing, the required values need to be entered onto the schedule of test results. Now we need to look at each of these tests in detail.

CONTINUITY OF PROTECTIVE CONDUCTORS

The equipment required for this test is a low-resistance ohm meter, which is capable of providing accurate readings

CONTINUITY OF MAIN PROTECTIVE BONDING

This test will require the use of a long test lead.

- Check that the installation is isolated from the supply.
- Disconnect one end of the protective bonding, usually easiest at the consumer's unit.
- Check that the test instrument is operating correctly and is accurate. Now measure the resistance of the leads being used for the test. The resistance of these leads will need to be subtracted from the final reading. Some instruments have a null function, which will allow for resistance of the leads to be automatically subtracted.
- Connect one test lead to the disconnected end of the main bonding conductor and the other test lead to the furthest point of the main bonding conductor.
- The measured value should be no greater than 0.05Ω after the resistances of the leads have been subtracted. A 10mm^2 conductor will need

Checking continuity of main equipotential bonding conductors for compliance with Regulation 612.2

As required by Regulation 544.1.2, the main equipotential bonding connection to any gas, water or other service shall be made as near as practicable to the point of entry of that service into the premises.

Where there is an insulating section or insert at that point, or there is a meter, the connection shall be made to the consumer's hard metal pipework and before any branch pipework.

Where practicable the connection shall be made within 600mm of the meter outlet union or at the point of entry to the building if the meter is external.

For copper or copper-equivalent, main equipotential bonding conductors the minimum cross-sectional area is 6 sq mm and subject to a maximum of 25 sq mm except for PME supplied installations where the minimum csa is in accordance with Table 54.8 of BS 7671

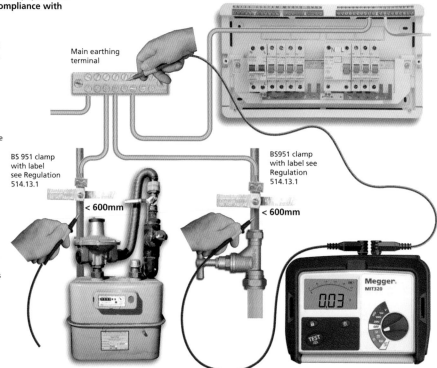

Long lead test for bonding conductor.

to be approximately 25m long before this value is reached. If the value is greater than 0.05Ω, then the cable may not be large enough. Always check the tightness of the lead connection and measure again before thinking about changing the size of the conductor.

- Reconnect the main protective bonding as soon as possible – this will avoid it being forgotten about.

CONTINUITY OF CIRCUIT PROTECTIVE CONDUCTORS (CPC)

This test will require the use of standard length leads, which of course will need to be nulled or the resistance subtracted from the final result.

- At one end of the circuit, join the line and CPC together. This is normally easiest at the consumer's unit and can be done with a short lead, which has crocodile clips on each end, or alternatively the ends can just be connected into the same terminal.

- A test between line and earth must now be carried out at each point to ensure that every outlet is correctly connected to earth. The highest value recorded will be the $R_1 + R_2$ for the circuit. This must now be entered into the column on the schedule of test results, which is marked as $R_1 + R_2$. The highest measured value should be from the outlet that is furthest in cable length from the consumer's unit or, if the link has been carried out at the furthest point, the highest value should be at the consumer's unit.

Method 1 for checking polarity, continuity, and measuring R1 + R2 for compliance with Regulation 612.2 and 612.6

Split-load Consumer Unit securely isolated from the supply, and proved to be so, before proceeding.

Make a temporary link between Phase and CPC. Make sure this link is removed before re-energising.

For lampholders having an earthed neutral conductor, centre contact bayonet or Edison screw lampholders having the outer or screwed contacts connected to the neutral conductor, polarity must be checked separately at the lampholder (except E14 and E27 lampholders to BS EN60238).

The CPC to the light switch should also be verified.

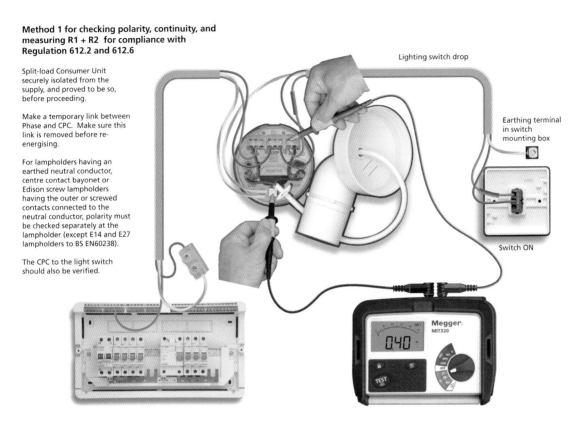

Lighting switch drop

Earthing terminal in switch mounting box

Switch ON

R1 + R2 test.

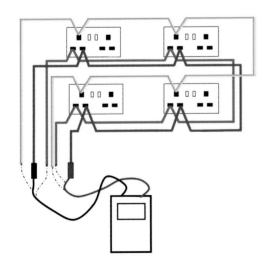

Measure each conductor resistance.

- Every radial circuit must be subjected to this test and the $R_1 + R_2$ value for it must be recorded in the appropriate row.

RING FINAL CIRCUIT TEST

This test is also carried out using a low-resistance ohm meter with nulled leads or the value of them must be subtracted at each step of the test.

All ends of the ring circuit must be disconnected at the consumer's unit, and each conductor must be measured end to end for resistance. This it to ensure that each conductor is connected at each outlet and forms a complete loop.

As an example, let's assume that the circuit is wired in 2.5mm^2 with a 1.5mm^2 CPC and that the

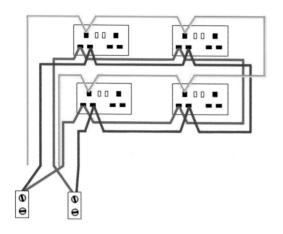

Cross-connect L–N of ring.

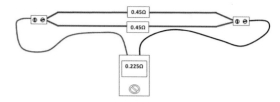

Conductors measured in parallel.

sectional area, which will halve the resistance again; this will give a resistance value of 0.225Ω.

Shown as a calculation:

$$\frac{0.45 + 0.45}{4} = 0.225\Omega$$

end-to-end resistance of the live conductors is 0.45Ω and a CPC resistance of 0.75Ω.

Now the line from one end of the cable (L1) must be connected to the neutral (N2) of the other end of the cable. Then the neutral (N1) must be connected to the (L1). This will form a complete loop.

Now the resistance can be measured across the two joined ends. This will show us the value that we should get when we measure between the line and neutral at each socket outlet. In this instance, the value should be:

L – L = 0.45Ω + N – N = 0.45Ω,

which, if added together in one length, will give a resistance value of 0.9Ω.

As these conductors are connected in a loop, we will be measuring half the length, which will have a resistance of 0.45Ω, and as the conductors are now in parallel, we will be measuring twice the cross-

The value may vary slightly but it should not vary by more than +/–0.05Ω. Also, you must make sure that the switch on each socket outlet is in the On position; if it is not you will not get a reading other than an open circuit.

The highest value measured will be the $R_1 + R_n$ value and some test result schedules do not need this value recorded, although it must always be measured.

Once each socket has been measured for the $R_1 + R_n$ value, the ends can be disconnected.

Now we must repeat the process with the line and earth of each end of the cables cross-connected just as we did with the L and N.

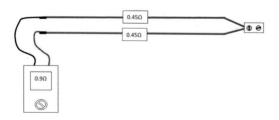

This measurement will be the same at each socket.

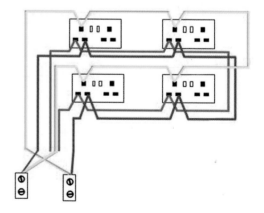

Cross-connect L–E.

Once the connections are made, a resistance value can be measured between the joined ends at the consumer's unit. As before this will give us an indication of the value we expect to measure at each outlet when we measure between line and earth.

For our example, the value will be the value of the line conductor added to the value of the CPC and then divided by 4:

$$\frac{0.45 + 0.75}{4} = 0.3\Omega$$

Now we must measure between line and earth at each outlet, remembering to subtract the lead resistance if we have not nulled the leads. Because the CPC is a different size to the line conductor, the resistance value will be very slightly less for the sockets that are near to the beginning and end of the ring, and will increase to 0.3Ω at the centre of the ring.

If the ring circuit has a spurred socket or fused connection unit, then the measured value will be higher than 0.3Ω due to the additional length of cable.

The highest value that is measured between the line and earth should be entered into the correct row for the ring circuit that has been tested. In our example, the value of $R_1 + R_2$ will be 0.3Ω.

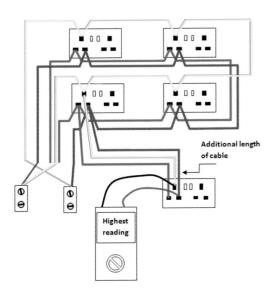

Additional resistance due to a spur.

On the schedule of test results there is a box to tick if the circuit is a ring. This must be ticked for a ring circuit and a line drawn through it if it is not a ring. There is also a column for polarity, where the ring test has been satisfactory, the polarity – box should also be ticked.

INSULATION RESISTANCE TEST

This test is doing exactly what it says – it is testing the resistance of the insulation. It is really important to ensure that there is no current leakage between the conductors of any circuit.

An insulation test is very similar to carrying out a pressure test on a water-filled central heating system to check for leaks. The difference is that we increase the pressure of our electricity in our circuit, whereas in a water-filled heating circuit we would increase the pressure of the water.

To carry out this test we need an insulation resistance tester. This is an instrument that will produce the voltage required to test the quality of the insulation between the conductors. The test voltage used is dependent on the voltage of the circuit that we are testing.

Values of voltage to be used.

Circuit voltage (V)	Test voltage (V) d.c.	Minimum insulation resistance (MΩ)
SELV and PELV 0V to 50V a.c.	250	0.5
Low voltage 50V to 500V a.c.	500	1.0
Above 500V a.c.	500	1.0

For a low-voltage circuit of between 50V and 500V, we must use a test voltage of 500V d.c.

Before the test can be carried out, the circuit must be prepared correctly; if it is not, one of two things will happen. If there is an item of current-using equipment connected to the circuit, the test will produce a bad reading, or if the equipment is sensitive, it may be damaged by the higher value of voltage used for the test.

For circuit preparation we must first ensure that there is no current-using equipment connected, which will include switching off fixed equipment, making sure that there are no neons in the circuit, removing light bulbs and even disconnecting some items such as fluorescents and lighting transformers.

We must also disconnect or bypass any equipment that may be vulnerable to damage, such as dimmer switches or motion sensors. Where this vulnerable equipment is being used as a switch, it must be bypassed or linked out so that all of the circuit is tested and not only tested up to the switch.

Once we have prepared the circuit we must make sure that all of the light switches are in the On position.

Before the test can be carried out, the test instrument and leads must be inspected visually for any damage. The leads must also comply with GS 38, as the test voltage used is over 50V.

Once you have verified that the instrument and leads are not damaged, the instrument must be checked for accuracy and correct operation. As with all electrical test instruments, the check for accuracy is ongoing and records of these checks should be kept. When an instrument is found to be inaccurate, it must be sent away for calibration.

Correct operation of the instrument checked by connecting the leads together and operating the test button, the reading on the instrument should be 0.00MΩ. The leads must now be disconnected and the test button pushed again; this time the reading should be as high as the instrument can read, possibly >200MΩ or even greater, depending on the type of instrument.

It is usually easier to carry out the test on the circuit at the consumer unit end, particularly when carrying out an initial verification, as all of the circuits can be tested without moving around too much.

Connect the test leads to the L and N of the circuit and operate the test button. The value should be very high for a new circuit, probably greater than the instrument can measure. If for some reason the value measured is less than 2MΩ, then further investigation is required as this could indicate that the circuit has a defect, which may in time become a problem. Although the regulations state that 1MΩ is acceptable, it would be very unusual to have value that low on a new circuit.

Dimmer bypassed.

Where this test is being carried out on a lighting circuit, it is important that the test is repeated when any two-way or intermediate switching is operated.

The value of the test results must now be entered onto the schedule of test results and the circuit reinstated ready for energizing.

POLARITY

A check for the correct polarity is required for all circuits, to ensure that every single pole switch and protective device is connected in the line conductor only, and that all ES lampholders, with the exception of E14 and E27 types, have the outer or screwed contacts connected to the neutral conductor.

A check must also be made to ensure that all wiring has been correctly connected to socket outlets, fused connection units and similar equipment.

Although the polarity check is listed to be carried out after the insulation tests, in most instances it is checked during the $R_1 + R_2$ test and the ring final circuit test, as it forms part of those tests.

The schedule of test results has a tick box for each circuit to indicate that the polarity is correct; this must be ticked for each circuit.

Once all of the dead tests have been carried out the system can be energized. However, it is always sensible, on an initial verification of an installation, to check that the supply from the meter is the correct polarity.

The test check should be carried out using an approved voltage indicator or test lamp to GS 38:

- Step 1. Test between the line and neutral and the device should indicate that there is a voltage present.
- Step 2. Test between the line and earth and the device should indicate that there is a voltage present.
- Step 3. Test between the neutral and earth and the device should indicate that there is *not* a voltage present.

Z_E TEST

A Z_e test is required to ensure that the system has an earth. The test can be carried out using the same method for all types of system, including a TT system.

The test is carried out using an earth fault loop impedance test instrument with leads to GS 38. Once again the instrument, as with all instruments, must be checked for damage, accuracy and correct operation before use.

The procedure for carrying out the test is as follows:

- Step 1. Isolate the installation from the supply; this can be achieved by switching off the main switch at the consumer's unit.
- Step 2. Disconnect the earthing conductor from the main earthing terminal inside the consumer's unit.
- Step 3. Connect the red lead of the instrument to the disconnected earthing conductor using a crocodile clip.
- Step 4. Place the probe of the green instrument lead onto the incoming line terminal at the main switch.
- Step 5. Take a reading and record the value onto the schedule of test results.

The value measured will be the Z_e for the installation. For a TT system it could be a high reading – any reading on this type of system that is over 200Ω will be unacceptable and the use of another electrode should be considered.

A TNS system should not have a value of greater than 0.8Ω and a TN-C-S system should not be greater than 0.35Ω.

Should the values of Z_e be greater than expected for a TN-S or A TN-C-S, then the distribution network operator should be consulted. However, in most cases it is easier to install an RCD, particularly on a new installation.

Once the test has been completed it is vital for safety reasons to ensure that the earthing conductor is reconnected as soon as possible.

PROSPECTIVE FAULT CURRENT (IpF)

Prospective fault current is the highest current that could possibly flow within the installation under fault conditions. We need to know the value of this current so as to ensure that we can select equipment that is suitable. In particular, we need to give special attention to protective devices.

To find out what the highest current is that could flow, we will need to carry out two tests: a prospective short circuit current test (PSCC) and a prospective earth fault current test (PEFC)

Both of these tests can be carried out with the supply connected and switched on.

Prospective Short Circuit Current

To carry out this test, a PSCC test instrument should be used, which is the same instrument that we use for PEFC. If it is a two-lead test instrument, the dial setting on the instrument will be the same for both tests and the two leads will be placed onto different terminals. If it is a three-lead instrument, the leads will remain connected but the instrument dial setting will be altered.

Two-Lead Instrument

Ensure that the instrument is undamaged, accurate and with leads to GS 38. Set the dial to PSCC and at the main switch place one of the probes onto the incoming line terminal and the other onto the neutral terminal. Take a reading and make a note of it. This value will be the prospective short circuit current for the installation.

Now place one of the leads onto the incoming line terminal and the other lead onto the main earth terminal, take a reading and make a note of it. This value will be the prospective earth fault current for the installation.

Three-Lead Instrument

Connect the instrument leads to the appropriate terminals at the main switch: red/brown lead to incoming line, black/blue lead to the incoming neutral and the green lead to the main earth terminal.

Set the instrument dial to PSCC, take a reading and make a note of it. Leave the test leads connected and set the instrument to PEFC and take another reading and make a note of it.

It does not matter if you did a two-lead or a three-lead test, the next part of the process is the same. The highest of the recorded values must be recorded as the prospective fault current I_{pf} on the schedule of test results.

All of the protective devices must now be checked to ensure that they are capable of interrupting the PFC without damage. This is done by comparing the I_{cn} of the device with the PFC. The I_{cn} must be greater than the PFC.

EARTH FAULT LOOP IMPEDANCE (Z_S)

The next part of the initial inspection is to check all of the circuit Z_s values. The instrument required for this test is an earth fault loop impedance test instrument.

Once again the instrument should be inspected and checked for accuracy.

This requires a test to be carried out at the end of the circuit that is furthest from the consumer's unit. On the schedule of test results you will have by now recorded Z_e for the system and the $R_1 + R_2$ value for each circuit. The test is carried out to ensure that the measured live Z_s value for the circuit is not greater than $Z_e + R_1 + R_2 = Z_s$.

When using a two-lead instrument:

- Turn off the circuit.
- At the furthest end of the circuit, connect the red test lead to the line conductor and the green test lead to the earth terminal.
- Re-energize the circuit and record the test value.
- Turn off the circuit and remove the leads, then replace any covers.

When using a three-lead instrument:

- Turn off the circuit.
- At the furthest end of the circuit connect the test leads to the appropriate terminals.
- Turn on the circuit and record the test value.
- Turn off the circuit and remove the leads, then replace the covers.

The next part of the process is the same for a two-lead and a three-lead test.

The first part of the check is to add the value of Z_e to the $R_1 + R_2$ value; this will give us the calculated Z_s. Now compare the measured value

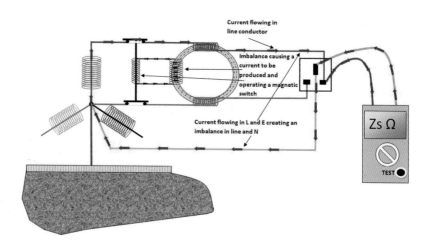

Current flowing in line conductor

Imbalance causing a current to be produced and operating a magnetic switch

Current flowing in L and E creating an imbalance in line and N

Zs Ω

TEST

Imbalance of current flow caused by an earth fault loop test.

against the calculated value. The calculated value of Z_s should not be higher than the measured value of Z_s.

The second part of the check is to compare the measured value of Z_s to the maximum permitted value of Z_s, which can be obtained from the correct table for the type of protective device being used. The measured value must not be greater than the maximum value.

If all is suitable, then the measured Z_s value should be recorded in the Z_s column for the circuit.

Whist it is always desirable to obtain the actual Z_s value for a circuit by direct measurement, this is often difficult to achieve when the circuit is protected by a residual current device. This is because during an earth loop impedance test a current is allowed to pass through the line conductor and the CPC. This, of course, creates an imbalance of the current flow between the line and CPC within the RCD. The imbalance could be up to 25A as this is the current at which the earth loop tester operates.

To overcome this problem it is possible to use an RCD tester, which uses a low current for the test. In most instances this will prevent the RCD from operating during the test.

Another method, which is quite acceptable, is to simply add the measured Z_e to the measured R_1 + R_2; this will give a calculated Z_s that can be entered onto the schedule of test results.

RCD TEST

This next test is to ensure that any RCDs installed operate within the required time. The test instrument used is called an RCD tester, and it is used to measure the time it takes for an RCD to operate and shut off the flow of current.

The test instrument must have leads that comply with GS 38. Leads can either have a plug top on, which will be used to test socket outlets, or it can have three probes, which can have crocodile clips connected to them if required.

To carry out the test we must first look to see which type of RCD is to be tested. For this test we need to know whether the RCD is a BS or a BS EN type, this is because they have different maximum disconnection times.

Before we start the test, we need to identify the type; most of the new types will be BS EN. We also need to know the trip current value of the device; the trip rating ($I_{\Delta n}$) for most domestic RCDs will be 30mA but always be sure to check.

An RCD with a trip rating ($I_{\Delta n}$) of up to and including 30mA must be tested at ×½ then ×1 and a final test of ×5. RCDs that have a trip rating of above 30mA must only be tested at ×½ and ×1, and not tested at ×5.

For an RCD that is protecting a socket outlet, we can simply plug the instrument in. We then need to set the instrument to match the rating of the RCD,

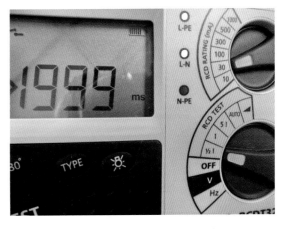

RCD tester with GS 38 leads.

RCD tester set at 15mA.

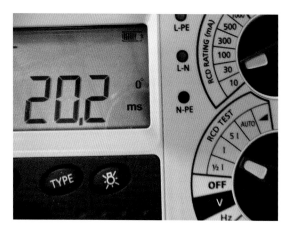

RCD test at ×1 and 0 degrees.

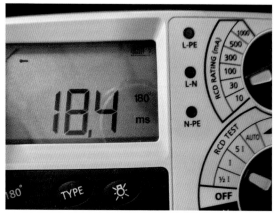

RCD test set at ×1 and 180 degrees.

e.g. 30mA for a 30mA RCD. Now the instrument must be set at x½.

Now we can push the test button and the RCD should not switch off within 2sec. The x½ test must be carried out on all RCDs regardless of $I_{\Delta n}$ value.

For the next part of the test, the instrument must be set at x1 of the trip rating ($I_{\Delta n}$) The test must be carried out on 0 degrees and 180 degrees and the maximum permissible trip time is 300ms for a BS EN type, and 200ms for a BS type, although in most cases the values obtained will be far less than the maximum permitted.

All RCDs of 30mA must also be tested at x5 the rating. Again the test must be carried out on 0 degrees and 180 degrees. The maximum discon-nection time for the ×5 test is 40ms for all types of RCD up to and including 30mA.

As a final check, the manual test button must be pushed to prove that the device is mechanically sound. Never push the button before carrying out the RCD test. It is also very important to ensure that the RCD test notice is attached next to the RCD – this is supposed to remind people to push the button every 3 months.

FUNCTIONAL TESTING

Functional testing must be carried out to ensure that all switches, circuit breakers and the RCD push-button operate correctly.

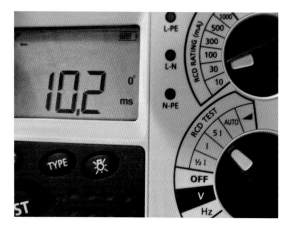

RCD test set at ×5 and 0 degrees.

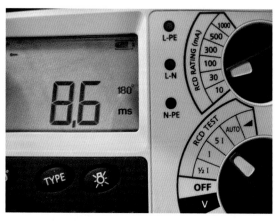

RCD test set at ×5 and 180 degrees.

Index

ambient temperature 130
anchor bolts 57
architrave box 63–64

bending spring 51
bonding 75
  clamps 88, 90
  continuity 149
building regulations 5
buried cables 126

cables 30–44
  buried 126
  connections 74, 107, 139
  current carrying capacity 131
  floors and ceilings 68
  lofts 72
  resistance 86, 132
  route 67
  stud partitions 73
  under floors 72
  walls and partitions 67
cable selection 129
calibration 154
capping 47
cartridge fuse 84
ceiling rose 107
chasing walls 50
circuits
  multiple 69
  protective conductors 82, 85, 98, 128
competent person 4
condition report inspection
    schedule 16–18

conduit 38
  boxes 65, 148
  circuit breaker 84, 132
  lighting circuits 91, 97
cooker point 119
cord switch 124

dimmer switch 99
distribution circuit 124
  remote building 126
diversity 120
domestic dwelling 4
double insulated cable 39
drilling joists 68, 71
dry wall box 46

earth electrode 82, 128
earth fault loop impedance 155
earthing 75, 81
electric shock 13, 85
electrical installation certificate 7, 143–145
electrical installation condition
    report 14–15
electricity 4
electricity at work regulations 4, 19
extra low voltage 28
extra low voltage lighting 103

FELV 28
fire hood 101
fire rated cables 44
fishing 72
fixings 53–60

flat multicore cable 30
flooring
  tongue and grooved 69
  chip board 70
functional testing 157
FP 200 44, 67
fuse
  rewirable 83
  cartridge 84
fused connection unit 108, 117

glazed tiles 56
grouping 130

Health and Safety at Work Act 4
Henley block 125
high tuff 39

immersion heater 122
initial verification 142
inspecting and testing 142
installation methods 45
insulation resistance 152
i_{pf} 154

joint boxes 74, 92, 99
joists 68
  drilling 71, 98
  notching 68, 71, 98

knock out box 47, 62–64

ladders 22
legal requirements 4

lighting circuits 91
  adding a point 93
  dimmer switch 99
  es lampholders 154
  extra low voltage 103
  intermediate switching 96
  junction box method 92
  loft light 111
  motion sensor 108
  new circuit 97
  no earth 112
  one way switching 91
  outside light 104, 110
  two-way switching 93

main protective bonding 88, 149
mains block 125
manual handling 20
masonry drill 56
microgeneration 134
mineral insulated cable 40, 67
mini trunking 40
minor works certificate 6
motion sensor 108

new circuit 5
no earth in a lighting circuit
  112
notching joists 68, 71

oval conduit 48

Part P 4, 5, 142
PELV 28
photovoltaic system 134
planning 66
plastic capping 47
  bending 52
  boxes 65
  oval 49
  plastic conduit 48
  round 50
  support 52
plasterboard wall
  box 62
  fixings 57–60
  stud partitions 73
plastic box 60–63
plastic plugs 56
power circuits 113

adding a socket 115
cooker point 119
immersion heater 122
outside socket 118
remote building 126
shower circuit 123
prospective short circuit current
  155
protective bonding 75, 87
  main 88
  supplementary 89
polarity 154

radial circuits 117
rating factors 129
rawl bolts 57
RCD 68, 82, 97, 119, 127, 157
reduced low voltage 29
regulations 4
remote building 126
ring final circuits 113
  testing 151
roof hooks 137

safe isolation 19
  flowchart 20
  procedure 20
scaffold 23
schedule of inspections 10, 143,
  146
schedule of test results 12, 148
screws 53
SDS chuck 26
SELV 28
semi enclosed rewirable fuse 83,
  129
shower 123
single conductors 38
socket outlets 113
  outside 118
solar cables 139
steel capping 47
steel wire armour cable 34–38,
  128
step ladders 21
stud partitions 73
supplementary bonding 89
sub-main 124
supply systems 75–81
  TT ,TN-S,TN-C-S 78–80

surface plastic box 60–63
surge protection 133
switching
  intermediate 96
  one way 91
  two way 93

telephone cables 69
testing 142
  continuity of CPC 150
  earth fault loop impedance z_s
    156
  functional testing 158
  insulation resistance 153
  polarity 154
  prospective short circuit current
    155
  RCD test 157
  ring final circuit 151
  z_e 82–87, 132, 155
thermal insulation 68, 72
TN-C-S system 79
TN-S system 79
toggle bolt 58
tools 24, 50
  hole saw 102
  pad saw 102
  stud finder 101
  wood drill bits 71
total load 120
tower scaffold 22
transformer 27
trunking 38
  mini 49
TT system 76, 82, 86, 128
twin and earth cable 30

voltage bands 27
voltage drop 124, 131

wiring
  lighting circuits 91
working at height 21
wood screws 53

z_e 82, 86, 149, 155
z_s 83, 85, 149
zones 45, 67